TRADE

A FIRESIDE BOOK
from Skylight Press
PUBLISHED BY SIMON & SCHUSTER
New York   London   Toronto   Sydney   Singapore

SECRETS

Winifred Conkling

Get the Most for Your Money—All the Time—on Goods and Services Ranging from Alarms and Art, Cars and Computers, to Financial Planning and Hotel Reservations

FIRESIDE
Rockefeller Center
1230 Avenue of the Americas
New York, NY 10020

Copyright © 1995 by Skylight Press
All rights reserved, including the right of
reproduction in whole or in part in any form.

FIRESIDE and colophon are registered trademarks
of Simon & Schuster Inc.

DESIGNED BY BARBARA M. MARKS

Manufactured in the United States of America

1   3   5   7   9   10   8   6   4   2

Library of Congress Cataloging-in-Publication
Data

Conkling, Winifred.
Trade secrets : get the most for your money—
all the time—on goods and services ranging
from alarms and art, cars and computers, to
financial planning and hotel reservations /
Winifred Conkling.
p.   cm.
''A Fireside book.''
1. Consumer education—United States.
2. Shopping—United States.   I. Title.
TX336.C64   1995
640'.73'0973—dc20   95-15791
                                       CIP

ISBN 0-684-81182-0

For Jonathan Rak
with love

Contents

Just think of all the really useful things you learned in school: algebra, the presidents of the United States in order, the names of the rivers in the former Soviet Union. What you probably *didn't* learn, but wish you had, was how to shop without getting ripped off, handle your finances without making dumb mistakes, and how to function as a professional consumer in a bewildering marketplace.

In fact, schools teach students how to *earn* a living but not how to get the most for their hard-earned money. We turn out amateur consumers to do battle with professional retailers, fraudulent telemarketers, and complex high-tech products and financial instruments that would baffle Einstein.

If you want to arm yourself to hold your own as a consumer, there is help available. *Consumer Reports* magazine publishes product test data and advice for buying products and services. Government-required disclosures, labels, and standards help you protect yourself if you take the time to read them. Sharp-eyed reading and questioning of contracts and fine print will save you from making big mistakes.

And now there is another way to brush up on your shopping savvy. *Trade Secrets* provides you with useful and amusing inside information that will give you an edge. Just because you are not in the trade, there's no reason you shouldn't know the tricks.

—Jean Ann Fox, president, Consumer Federation of America

Introduction

What do you do when your kitchen sink backs up? You call Uncle Fred the plumber to help bail you out. You decide it's time to indulge yourself and buy that strand of cultured pearls. So you put in a call to Aunt Joan, the jeweler, and get a few pointers on picking out the most lustrous pearls for the best price. It's finally time to take the plunge and buy life insurance. Rather than throw yourself at the mercy of an unknown insurance salesperson, you call Uncle Rodger and he sells you the right policy at the right price.

Sounds great, doesn't it? But how many of us have a family that's big enough—or talented enough—to provide worthwhile advice on a variety of topics? Never fear. *Trade Secrets* will let you in on the tricks of the trade, just as if you had an uncle in the biz, and will help you save money, recognize value, and buy the very best product for your money. And to help guide you through the decision-making process, special sections are provided:

- *That's Bull* warns you about the less-than-truthful claims manufacturers and salespeople sometimes make;
- *Key Lingo* defines some of the common terms used in the field so that you can talk like a pro;
- *Advice Is Cheap* tips you off about the advice you're apt to hear from salespeople and friends that isn't necessarily wrong—just wrong for your particular needs;
- *Don't Forget to Ask* lists questions you should ask before putting down any money; and

- ***Trivia to Impress Your Friends*** provides fascinat-
  ing tidbits of information that will make you an interesting guest at any cocktail party.

  Without help, you could spend a lifetime learning the
tricks of the trade the hard way—by trial and error. Instead,
enjoy the expert advice scores of insiders provided for this
book. Every business has its secrets; the time has now come
to let you in on them. No more deception, no more falling
for stale marketing ploys. Let me tell you about the tricks
of the trade . . .

Chapter One

DOING
YOUR HOME WORK

■ BUYING PEACE OF MIND:
CHOOSING THE BEST BURGLAR ALARM

Common sense tells you that if a burglar is debating whether to break into your house, equipped with a home security system, or break into your neighbor's unprotected house, your neighbor is in trouble. Recent studies have backed this up, finding that burglars strike unprotected homes five to six times more often than homes with electronic alarm systems. Such deterrence is one of the best reasons to go through the hassle of installing an alarm system.

Face it: These days a lock isn't enough. FBI figures show that more than 80 percent of the time, a burglar gets into your home through a door, most often the front door. Sometimes the bad guys smash down the door; if they confront a deadbolt or double lock, they'll often use the "international passkey"—a crowbar—to take out the entire door frame.

Alarm systems come with both eyes and ears: Some systems have audio sensors that listen for the sound of breaking glass; others shoot invisible infrared beams across the room, waiting for some unsuspecting burglar to cross the beam. Still other systems have sensors at strategic points that trip the alarm if the contact is broken by opening a wired door or window.

So, how much do you have to pay for security? For a complete setup with sensors at all the doors and windows,

Key Lingo

When you're exploring your options, don't be alarmed by the industry lingo:

Audio sensor: *A device used near windows that listens for the audio frequency of the sound of breaking glass. This system works best when there isn't a lot of background noise.*

Central station system: *An alarm that sends a signal over special phone lines directly to a monitoring post or the police or fire department. This system alerts the police if the phone line has been cut and can save time in an emergency.*

Digital dialer alarm: *An alarm that sends the same signals to the police and fire department but uses the regular phone lines. If your phone line has been cut or if you're on the phone, the call can't go through.*

Hardwired system: *An alarm system that actually has a series of wires that run from the door or window to a central box in a closet or basement. These systems work well and are the most common devices used in homes.*

Long-range radio alarm: *A system that sends the alarm signal to the central station by radio signal. This system avoids the risk of a cut phone line, but it requires frequent tests to make sure it works properly.*

Pet alley: *The space between the floor and the infrared beam used to monitor movement inside the house. By setting the beam about three or four feet off the ground, the dog or cat has room to wander without tripping the alarm.*

Wireless system: *An alarm system that uses radio transmitters (like those in garage-door openers) stationed by every window and door to send radio waves to a central box elsewhere in the house. If you object to living with little plastic boxes throughout your house, choose a hardwired system.*

you'll pay an average of $1,700 for installation plus about $20 a month for the security company to monitor the alarm and contact the police if the alarm goes off. A small price to pay for peace of mind, right? You can make those alarm-dollars go farther by keeping certain issues in mind when shopping for a system.

Go ahead, wake the neighbors. Pick a noisy system that will shout first and ask questions later. Look for an alarm with sirens, buzzers, or bells—no need to be shy and retiring—so the burglar will know he's been found out and that the police will be arriving shortly.

Burglars do windows. Don't cheap out and put sensors on only a couple of doors or windows. You need to keep an electronic eye on your entire house. Some discount systems offer only a limited number of contact points, often three. Unless you have only one door and two windows, this isn't enough protection.

Beyond burglars. Many alarm systems combine fire and burglar alarms. For about $100 to $250 more, your alarm system can provide fire protection, too. Like common smoke and heat detectors, these systems scream *"Fire,"* but they go one step farther and call the fire department for you. When time is of the essence, those minutes saved by alerting the fire department right away can make the difference in saving your possessions—and perhaps even your life. (If you burn something in the kitchen and trigger a false alarm, you can call the alarm service before the fire trucks arrive screaming to your front door.) In addition, some burglar-plus systems also keep a lookout for frozen pipes, natural gas leaks, and stand guard in case of medical emergencies.

Protect your house inside and out. In addition to the door and window sensors monitoring the perimeter of the house, choose a system that will watch what's going on inside. Indoor activity can be monitored using thin electronic pressure pads that are slipped under the rug or carpet or infrared beams that trigger an alarm when they sense the movement of an object with a temperature of 98 degrees or higher. Other systems use photoelectric beams, ultrasonic and microwave systems, as well as other motion detectors. Many alarms come with a feature that allows you to activate either an "at home" setting, which sets the alarms on the doors and windows but leaves you free to move around the house at night, or an "away" setting, which turns on the entire system, including the indoor motion detectors.

Don't cry wolf with too many false alarms. Some cities ticket you if the police are called to your address more than two or three times on false alarms. In certain cases, you might have to have the alarm system serviced by the dealer before the police will respond to any more calls. Nobody's perfect; if you have an alarm you can expect a few false alarms, so just try to keep the number down.

Let me see your badge. Well, at least let me see your state business license. The last thing you want to do is invite a con artist or prospective burglar into your home to assess its security weaknesses. Before you allow any alarm representative into your home, and before you answer specific questions over the phone, demand proof of licensure.

Don't Forget to Ask

☐ *Are you licensed by the state?*
☐ *How long have you been in business?*
☐ *Who will monitor the system? Is that work subcontracted?*
☐ *Will this alarm system qualify for a discount on my homeowner's insurance policy?*
☐ *What are the maintenance fees?*
☐ *Is there a penalty for false alarms?*
☐ *May I have a list of previous customers?*

Don't be shy about posting alarm stickers.
Some would-be burglars won't bother with a house with an
alarm—or even an alarm sticker. Some companies simply
sell stickers for a nominal charge; others sell stickers for
about $1,500—then offer to throw in a free alarm system!
Serious burglars can spot a bogus sticker, but the warning
may be enough to intimidate the novice intruder.

■ IF IT AIN'T BROKE . . . BUT WHAT IF IT IS?

We are all well acquainted with the old adage "If it ain't
broke, don't fix it"—but what do we do when it *is* broken?
Every year millions of toasters, hair dryers, refrigerators,
VCRs, and other appliances large and small simply conk out.
It seems frightfully wasteful to discard broken-down goods,
but it's also tough to find an able, affordable, and honest
person to do the repairs. Fix-it shops are few and far between, and high-tech appliances often defy simple, low-cost
repairs.

It lived a good life. Or maybe not. But the general
rule of thumb is to give up on an appliance when the repairs
not covered by the warranty will cost 50 percent or more
of the replacement cost. The product warranty should cover
the item in its youth; you'll have to consider the life expectancy of the appliance when deciding if it has entered old
age. Keep in mind that most appliances either break down
early (when they're under warranty) or late (when they're
tired and thinking about retirement anyway).

Call in a specialist. If you decide to have an item
repaired, stick to an "authorized" service center for anything other than the most basic work. These folks have been

accredited by the company to do repairs, which should mean that they are familiar with the brand and model of your appliance, and they should have access to the appropriate parts.

There's no such thing as a free repair. On the other hand, maybe there is. A lot of credit card companies extend the term of your product warranty when you purchase merchandise with their card. Before throwing an item away or paying to have it repaired, check your credit card agreement and see if you can get it fixed on the credit card company's dime.

That's Bull

You just got a great deal on a new VCR and the sales rep is putting on the pressure to buy an extended warranty. When he says: "These things break down all the time. Don't you want the peace of mind?" tell him flatly: "No, I like to worry."

Extended warranties on appliances and electronic goods are basically a waste of money. More than four out of five people who buy them never use them even for maintenance and cleaning. For those who do file claims, the repair costs tend to be relatively low—compared to the cost of the policy. For every dollar spent on the warranties, less than 15 cents goes to pay for repairs; that's 85 cents going straight into the retailer's pocket. Think about it: If extended warranties weren't so profitable, the salespeople wouldn't be pushing them so hard, now would they?

Don't Forget to Ask

*Before asking for a repair person to come to your home for large
appliance repairs, be sure to ask the following:*

☐ *What is the "trip charge" or "house call" fee? (Expect to
pay $30 to $50 just to get a repair person to arrive at your
doorstep.)*

☐ *Will I be billed by the hour? The quarter hour?*

☐ *How long will the repair take?*

☐ *What is the warranty on the repair work? On the parts?*

☐ *Will I be able to keep the replaced parts? (Of course you don't
want to keep the broken belts and piles of greasy washers, but
asking to see the parts provides some assurance that the parts
you're being billed for are actually replaced.) One exception:
computer repairs. The repair person will often take the broken
component and return it to the manufacturer, who will refur-
bish it and sell it again. The repair person has an obligation
to tell you if you're receiving used components, even though
the warranty will be the same for the repair work.*

■ FIVE SECRETS OF SPOTTING QUALITY KITCHEN CABINETS

Whether constructed of solid wood, Formica, or polyurethane, your kitchen cabinets should last for decades with
little more than regular cleaning and periodic reorganization
—as long as you buy quality cabinets in the first place.
"Quality" doesn't have to mean "custom" cabinets. In
most cases you only need to buy custom cabinets if the
standard sizes won't fit in your kitchen; custom cabinets are
built to order.

Of course, you can go out of your way to spend huge sums of money on cabinets shimmering with a hand-rubbed finish, but such cabinets won't necessarily last longer or perform better than well-made standard ones. On the other hand, if you want serviceable cabinets on the cheap, stick to laminated pressed-plywood. They'll do the job and look . . . well, serviceable. What you pay depends on the look you choose: You could do a ten-by-ten-foot kitchen with pressed-wood cabinets and white laminated surfaces for less than $1,000, or you could easily spend $5,000 for custom oak cabinets for the same size kitchen.

Whatever your budget or aesthetic priorities, before ordering the cabinets for your remodeled kitchen, ask these five questions:

1. Have the cabinets earned the "seal of approval"? You thought your kids were hard on kitchen cabinets? Sure, kids slam the doors and hang on the drawers, but as part of its certification program, the Kitchen Cabinet Manufacturers Association puts them through worse. To test the finish, cabinets are covered with vinegar, lemon, orange and grape juices, tomato catsup, coffee, olive oil, and 100-proof alcohol. To assess door strength, a 65-pound weight is attached to the door as it swings back and forth ten times. In addition, those poor doors are opened and closed 25,000 times. (Maybe your children could get a summer job testing cabinets. . . .) Only those cabinets that pass muster earn the right to put a little blue-and-white "KCMA Certified Cabinet" sticker on the inside of the cabinet.

2. Are the interiors coated? Skip the shelf liner. Instead, look for cabinets with the interiors laminated with Formica, vinyl, or plastic-coated paper. No need to fuss with scissors and rolls of adhesive papers; just pick up a sponge and wipe out the crumbs and unidentified gook when the need arises.

3. Do the drawers have ball bearings? Feel the guide of the drawers. To avoid drawers that stick and jump off their tracks, settle for nothing less than ball-bearing rollers, which make the drawers open and close smoothly.

4. Are the corners fitted? Sturdier cabinets have grooved and glued joints rather than corners where one piece of wood simply abuts another, joined by hot glue and a nail or two.

5. Do the cabinets match my lifestyle? It makes no sense to pay twice the price for solid maple cabinets if you have a house full of toddlers who will gnaw on the doors and scribble on the cabinets.

That's Bull

Don't buy the line "A lazy Susan will make all your cabinets more efficient." A corner cabinet with a built-in lazy Susan can provide easy access to hard-to-reach corners, but in flat cabinets they only waste space.

■ ON THE LEVEL: HIRING A HOME CONTRACTOR

There are no two ways about it: Having work done in your house is stressful. It disturbs your nest, disrupts your daily routine, and defeats all attempts at keeping your house in order. If you're going to go to all the trouble and expense of hiring someone to work on your house, you're going to want the job done right—the first time. The following are things to do when hiring a home contractor that will increase your chances of being satisfied.

Check out the competition. Collect bids from at least three contractors that have been referred by friends or other reliable sources. In comparing bids, make sure the job specifications are the same; you don't want to hire a contractor only to learn that the quoted price didn't include all the work you need to have done. Beware of super-low bids: The contractor may be cutting corners somewhere.

Get nosy. You have a right to check out the contractor you've decided to use. Ask the contractor to provide proof of worker's compensation and liability insurance to cover injury to the workers as well as damage to your property. Call the state board of contractors to find out if the contractor is licensed and bonded. (A bond is money guaranteed by the contractor to cover only limited protection; it could not cover a large number of claims if a contractor was delinquent.) Licensing and bonding aren't guarantees of competence—some states grant licenses to anyone willing to pay for bonding—but you will be able to weed out those contractors whom you know you *don't* want working on your house.

Beware of the Fine Print

Keep in mind, when you hire a contractor, that it's your house on the line—or on the lien as the case may be. Contractors don't warn you about this potential liability, but if the contractor fails to pay his or her employees, subcontractors, or suppliers, these people have a legal right to put a lien on your house unless you cover the unpaid bills.

What can you do about it? Make sure that your contract includes a "hold harmless" or a general indemnification clause that says if you make your payments on time and in full, then you are free of any additional financial obligations. Before you sign a contract for a major renovation, check with a lawyer to make sure you're protected.

Don't Forget to Ask

☐ Does the contract specify the exact materials that will be used, including brand names?

☐ Does the contract include a work schedule? A date the job will start? A completion date? Is there a penalty for each day the work drags on beyond the stated completion date?

☐ Does the contract specify that the contractor will handle all cleanup?

☐ What kind of guarantee do you provide? For how long? (The manufacturer guarantees the cabinet or sink or other item being installed, but you need a guarantee from the contractor to cover the workmanship and proper installation.)

☐ How will any potential disputes be handled? Will we go to arbitration? Small claims court? (Make sure this is agreed to up front and noted in the contract.)

☐ Are you licensed by the state? Bonded?

☐ What kind of insurance do you carry to protect your workers? To protect my home?

☐ Does the contract include a "hold harmless" clause?

☐ Do you have any references? Can I see your work?

Be painfully specific. Make sure your written contract spells out every detail about the job: the exact materials that will be used, the work schedule, the timing of the payments. No one has ever regretted being too clear in a business agreement. It goes without saying: Never sign a contract with any blank spaces in it. (Write void or draw a line through the blank, if necessary.)

Hold onto your money as long as possible. You'll probably have to pay a deposit when you sign a contract, but you shouldn't have to pay more than one-third of the cost of the job. Withhold as much of the payment as possible until the work is finished; once the contractor has your money, there's no incentive to make sure you're satisfied.

If you change your mind, change the contract. As the job progresses, you may decide to switch to another color paint or a different cabinet design. That's fine, but you need to keep these changes formal. Get all the additional costs in writing before making any changes.

Watch the fine print. Make sure your written agreement explicitly states that the contractor is responsible for negligence or inferior work on the part of any subcontractors. You want to be able to say "That's *your* problem" if the contractor claims to have had difficulty with a certain subcontractor or employee.

■ DON'T JUST SIT THERE: FINDING FURNITURE

When it comes to buying furniture, you will literally have to live with the choices you make. So before putting any money down, take the time to research your options and find exactly what you want. You can save yourself time and trouble by following the Ten Commandments of Furniture Buying.

1. Know thy retailer. Buying a couch isn't like buying a tube of lipstick; you're spending a lot of money on an item that you'll be living with for many years. You need to know who you're doing business with. When ordering a piece of furniture, you often sign a contract and make a deposit, you're entering into a noncancelable agreement; the furniture is being made to order for you. Stick with a retailer with a good, long-standing reputation. If you buy from stock, you can see what you're buying ahead of time, but you still need to make sure the retailer will deliver the goods on time and take care of any problems that might arise.

2. Know thy likes and dislikes. If you don't know what you want, you're bound to get confused. There are literally thousands of furniture companies, each with many fabric and color options available. If you aren't sure exactly what ''look'' you're after, take the time to browse through furniture stores and to flip through magazines before starting your serious shopping.

3. Follow thy heart. Buying furniture isn't as academic as buying a washer or dryer. The way you furnish and decorate your home is an expression of your personality and style. Some people go for comfort, others for a formal look. You also need to sit down, take a load off, and find out what type of furniture feels right. Go ahead and let a little emotion creep into the decision-making process; otherwise you'll end up with a cookie-cutter living room that looks just like the showroom.

4. Fondle thy fabrics. And ask a lot of questions. There are tens of thousands of fabrics available for upholstered furniture, and there's no way anyone can become familiar with all of them. Natural fibers such as cotton and wool and silk feel fabulous, but they usually don't wear as well as synthetics. Often blended fabrics combine durability with softness. Touch, touch, touch. And ask about wear, colorfastness, and signs of wear. Borrow a fabric swatch and do the pencil test: Push the point of a pencil through the fabric and pull it out. If you can see a hole, the weave is too loose and won't wear well. (Please, don't do this on a display couch.)

5. Choose thy colors carefully. In general, dark colors with prints or patterns hold up to wear and tear better than light-colored solids. Look for fabrics that can be steam-cleaned or shampooed. Fabrics that require dry cleaning may not withstand heavy-duty family use. Unless the fabric comes pretreated, consider using a fabric-protective coating to minimize stains and allow easier cleaning.

6. Research thy hidden components. You can't see inside a piece of furniture to compare the quality of the frame, but you can ask the retailer and read the catalogs. High-quality frames are made of hardwoods or metal. This skeletal structure can make the difference between a top-notch recliner and its low-cost look-alike.

7. Prepare to wait for thy special orders. It's too expensive for a retailer to have in stock every piece of furniture in every fabric option. When you place an order, expect to wait several weeks or months for the furniture to be made to order. Some manufacturers guarantee quick delivery, but they may offer fewer choices of style and fabric. When you order the furniture, be sure to find out exactly how long it should take for the furniture to be finished and shipped to you. To avoid additional delays, ask whether the fabric you have chosen is in stock.

8. Prepare to wait even longer for thy special-order wooden furniture. For a manufacturer to cut a particular size or style of wooden table, the equipment must be set up and aligned to meet certain specifications. Since the manufacturer can't afford to realign the equipment each time a new order comes in, there can be a considerable wait for custom wood furniture. For example, a particular table may be cut only once a year. Patience in this case is a necessary virtue.

9. Visualize thy entire room. Some people have a lot of trouble taking tiny fabric swatches and visualizing the entire room. What looks good in a four-inch square may not look so great on a six-foot couch. Will you love it in the morning? If you're not too good at visualizing patterns, ask the salesperson to help you find out, either by finding pictures of furniture worked up in the fabric of your choice, or by using a video catalog, which allows you to see a computer-generated print-out of how the furniture would look covered with your chosen pattern.

10. Don't pay thy bill until fully satisfied. Whether you buy furniture off the floor, from showroom stock, or by special order, wait until the goods have been delivered and you have a chance to look them over before settling your accounts. Once the retailer has your money, you've lost most of your leverage.

Don't Forget to Ask

Before placing an order or buying from a showroom, give any piece of furniture a careful once-over. Get answers to the following questions:

☐ *Is the furniture stable when you gently push down on a top corner or press against the side?*

☐ *Is the back panel inset of dressers and wood furniture attached with screws or nails, which can pull out?*

☐ *Do the drawers and doors glide smoothly?*

☐ *Are the corners of the drawers joined with dovetail joints?*

☐ *Do long shelves have center braces?*

☐ *Are table leaves well supported?*

☐ *Are the hinges strong and well secured?*

■ LIVING IN "PLASTIC" HOUSES: DO YOU NEED A HOME-EQUITY LOAN?

You've undoubtedly heard the pitch: "Own your own home? Need cash? Have we got a deal for you!" Home-equity loans have become an increasingly flexible means for homeowners to get their hands on substantial amounts of cash, but you should keep in mind that they are really a second mortgage on your house.

Home-equity loans involve borrowing against the equity you have in your home. You can either take the money in a lump sum or use either a credit card or checks to slowly draw down the amount of equity. The money is considered a loan, and the interest rate is usually lower—perhaps as much as one or two percentage points lower—than it would be for a routine personal loan. Some lenders will even allow you to borrow at prime rate.

Borrowing against the equity in your house can be a cost-efficient and reasonable, perhaps even the only, way to get your hands on money you might need to pay college tuition or cover a large medical bill. Under certain conditions, the interest you pay may also be tax-deductible.

Risky business. Sounds like a great deal, but there are pitfalls—big ones. Keep in mind that you are using your home as collateral on the loan. This might make sense if you're house-rich and cash-poor, but if you lose your job, encounter unforeseen expenses, or otherwise overextend yourself and you can't repay the loan as planned, you could lose your home. Got that? *Lose your home.*

The sky's the limit. Actually, the limit is the amount of equity you have in your house. The equity is the appraised value, minus the amount owed on the first mortgage. Most lenders will give you only up to about 75 or 80 percent of the full amount (just in case real estate values drop).

I'd give my right arm for a Caribbean cruise. An arm maybe, but would you give up your home? You should consider carefully how you plan to use the money before taking out a home-equity credit line. Forgo the frivolous purchases, which can slowly erode the lifetime equity in your house. Is that vacation really worth putting your house on the line? Would you take out a personal loan to go on the same vacation?

That's Bull

Forget the smoke and mirrors. When it comes to making payments, there's one truth: Your house is going to cost more if you borrow money by taking out an equity loan. Even those deals that consolidate your monthly payments so you'll pay less each month don't tell the whole story; what the lenders forget to mention is that you'll be making payments for a longer period of time, so your total interest payments will go up. There's no such thing as a free lunch—or a free loan.

You better shop around. If you want a good deal, that is. There are a wide range of types of home-equity loans available at a wide range of interest rates and terms. For example, some lenders may allow you to pay only the interest on a loan for a certain length of time, say ten years. The advantage is lower monthly payments since you don't have to pay principal, but you may have to pay an interest rate that's somewhat higher than you would for an interest-plus-principal loan.

Break out your crystal ball. It's time to anticipate future interest rates. Do you want to choose a fixed-rate or a variable-rate loan? Usually, the initial interest rate is higher on a fixed-rate loan, but you have a guarantee that your rate won't go up, even if interest rates rise significantly. If you're taking out a loan and plan to pay it back over the long term, consider the fixed-rate loan. You can always refinance if interest rates drop markedly.

Losing control. Fixed interest rates may be available for lump-sum loans, but most home-equity credit lines require a variable interest rate. If you take out a loan and then interest rates rise, you might get stuck with higher monthly payments than you anticipated. Some loans have interest rates of a whopping 18 percent or more. Don't cry to the lender; a deal's a deal as far as the bank is concerned.

Don't mean to pop your bubble. Or your balloon, but balloon loans can be dangerous. These loans have low payments for three to five years, then the balance comes due. The monthly payments might be a snap, but if you can't come up with payment in full when the loan comes due, then you can lose your home. Never, never, never sign a contract for a balloon loan that doesn't allow you to renew the loan.

Don't assume that you could simply refinance the loan with another bank. For one thing, you won't know what the interest rates will be at the time you need to refinance, and for another, you could face significantly higher payments. Another issue: You could experience a change in your financial status—you could lose your job or face mounting medical bills—and you might not be able to get a new loan. It's not worth the risk.

Staying close to home. Some lenders are willing to put a home-equity or second mortgage behind their own first mortgage with you, and may offer a lower interest rate or other bonuses. If you're content with how the lender who holds your first mortgage is handling the account, then ask what kind of deal you can receive on an equity loan.

Too poor to rest. So you were planning to retire at age sixty-five. You figured the mortgage would be paid off and your monthly expenses would drop—but not if you take out a home-equity loan. Before taking out a loan, consider the long-term payment schedule not just in years— many loans extend over thirty years—but in terms of your age at different times during the repayment period. Unless you want to be eighty-five and still making payments on your house, keep this in mind.

When Refinancing Is Better

Sometimes you're better off starting over from scratch. Instead of taking out a separate home-equity loan, you may want to refinance the existing mortgage on your house.

Of course, it all depends on the interest rate you are paying on your mortgage. If you bought your house when interest rates were sky high, you may want to refinance at lower rates. However, if the interest rate on your existing mortgage is lower than the rates you can get today, you want to hold onto your mortgage—it's as good as money in the bank. Most experts agree that you shouldn't consider refinancing a mortgage unless the current interest rate is two percentage points below the rate of your existing mortgage.

■ PLUNGING IN: PICKING A PLUMBER

Most people don't like plumbing repairs: They don't know what's lurking in those clogged drains or backed-up toilets —or worse, they do. As a result, many a professional plumber earns a fair living retrieving Noxema jars, G.I. Joe dolls, and toddler training pants from stopped-up toilets.

If you have a problem that you can't fix yourself with a bottle of Drano or a trusty plunger, then it's time to seek professional help. Expect to pay handsomely for the house call: Most plumbers charge $25 to $50 an hour, more in urban areas. Before making an appointment, ask if there's a minimum fee or if you'll be charged the hourly rate even if the job takes just two or three minutes.

When it comes to serious waterworks, settle for nothing less than a Master Plumber. Look for someone who is licensed, bonded, and insured. In the plumbing hierarchy there are three levels of professionals: the apprentice (still wet behind the ears), the journeyman (a skilled tradesman who has spent four years as an apprentice and has passed an exam), and the master (a top-of-the-line plumber who has two additional years of experience and has earned a ''master's degree'' by passing another exam).

For a leaky faucet or a sink that won't drain, you'll do just fine hiring a handyman or general fix-it man, but don't trust a novice to do any jobs requiring a piping change or the installation of a major appliance, such as a water heater or a dishwasher. Sure, you probably can save a few dollars by seeking less-skilled help, but if the job is done wrong and your house burns down as a result, your homeowner's insurance carrier may not pay the claim.

Sounds dramatic, but every year hot water heaters explode because they are improperly installed without pressure-relief valves. When the thermostat fails—and it will some day—the heater stays on, and the water gets hotter and the pressure builds until the entire device blows like a nuclear bomb.

Less-experienced plumbers and do-it-yourselfers also have trouble with the venting procedures used in plumbing. If you have an improperly vented sink, you may wind up with sewer gas up your nose, a problem that is not only unpleasant but potentially dangerous.

Finding a qualified plumber can be as easy as opening the Yellow Pages. Start by calling those companies that have gone to the trouble to take out large-space ads. These companies want service work; they don't mind dealing with

That's Bull

Things never seem to go wrong at the right time. The sink always backs up on a Friday afternoon before a three-day weekend. The disposal invariably breaks down the day your dinner party is scheduled. When the pressure's on, you're in no shape to protest or second-guess your plumber's advice.

While most aren't out to sell you a new kitchen sink when all you need is a set of new washer rings, there are, of course, some unscrupulous plumbers. Lines to watch out for:

☐ **"This won't happen again if you buy a . . . "** The tradesman-turned-salesman now tries to sell you a strainer for the kitchen sink for $25 when you can find the identical item in any hardware store for a mere $3. The markup covers the plumber's overhead—plus a tidy profit (consider it a fee for home delivery). Save the money, shop for yourself.

☐ **"Do you want me to fix this other problem as long as I'm under the sink?"** When you call a plumber for a $50 job and you're told there's another $100 worth of repairs needed, get a second opinion. If a problem exists, you'll already have at least two estimates on getting it repaired.

☐ **"I don't usually do this kind of work . . . "** Stop. Plumbers who specialize in certain tasks tend to do them faster and with fewer complications than plumbers with expertise in other plumbing chores. For example, plumbers who fix faucets all day probably get the job done faster than those who usually work on home construction. Since you're probably paying by the hour for service or repair work, you'll save money—and time—by sticking with someone who specializes in the job you need to have done.

hysterical homeowners. The small ads are typically for plumbers who work with contractors and home builders and don't depend on clogged toilets for a living. Go ahead and call three or four companies, but you'll almost certainly find they all charge about the same rates.

You can save money and hassle by avoiding plumbing problems in the first place. First, set the thermostat on your hot water heater back to 120 degrees. Hotter water shortens the life of the heater. It's also much more dangerous; you can get a third-degree burn in a matter of seconds from water heated to 150 degrees.

Second, heat a couple of gallons of water to boiling on the stove and pour it down the drains every couple of weeks. This will go a long way toward clearing clogged drains by dissolving the grease and soap that glues the gook together causing the plug. No plug, no problem. No problem, no plumber.

■ How to Get the Red Carpet Treatment When Buying Carpet

When buying carpet, most people shop by color and cost. Alas, these poor folks may end up with floor covering unworthy of a barefoot stroll or unable to fend off an everyday spill or stain. When it comes to buying carpet, don't scrimp on quality, especially in high-traffic areas, or your floor will look matted, dirty, and worn in no time.

So what do you value in a carpet? Ultimately, the choice of carpet fiber—one of the first decisions you'll face—depends on how tough you plan to be on it. If you prize luxurious feel and resilience, go for a fine wool carpet, the standard against which all synthetics are compared. Wool resists stains and burns, cleans up easily, and grows old gracefully. No wonder it's the most expensive fiber, easily priced at two to three times the cost of the synthetics.

If wool is too costly, as it is for most people since it accounts for well under 5 percent of the entire market, a high-quality nylon carpet may do the trick. Of course, all nylons are not created equal. In general, nylon carpets are durable, resist dirt, resist static electricity, and can look a lot like wool. Those attributes apply, of course, to quality nylon carpets; inexpensive ones can appear shiny and cheap.

Other options include polyester, a common fiber used in deep-pile carpets but one that's less resilient than nylon and not as easy to clean. Unless you're carpeting a patio or utility room, you probably don't want to choose polypropylene (olefin), the standard fiber used in indoor/outdoor carpets. They certainly serve an important function in the carpet world—they resist color fading, they're a snap to clean, and they dry quickly because the fibers don't absorb moisture—but you probably don't want an olefin carpet in the living room since they have something of an industrial look and feel. It's the kind of carpet that might line the hallway in your doctor's office, not the kind of carpet you would want to lie on when snuggling on the floor in front of the fireplace.

That's Bull

Some carpet manufacturers brag that their carpets consist of "antimicrobial" nylon. Sounds good, except that bacteria, mold, mildew, and fungi—the invisible villains—don't grow on synthetic fibers. Instead, these microbial mischief-makers thrive on the dirt and spills left in the carpet. Clean up after spills and you won't need to worry about specially treated fibers.

Go ahead, wiggle your toes. Now it's time to let your personality show. Do you want a thick velvety carpet or a short nubby crew cut? You have a wide range of textures to choose from (see box below). Unless your carpet dealer has some *really* old stock in the back, you won't be able to find that good ole shag carpet so popular in the 1960s. Too bad.

A Matter of Style

Carpet manufacturers have a language all their own. This glossary of textures will help you appreciate the subtle differences in carpet design:

Berber: *A type of level-loop pile that has low rather than fat loops.*

Frieze: *A cut pile with fibers so tightly twisted that they turn over, creating a rough, nubby texture that wears well.*

Level loop: *Pile that has uncut loops of yarn, giving it a pebbly texture.*

Multilevel loop: *Also pile with uncut loops of varying heights.*

Plush *or* **velvet:** *Carpet with a smooth, even-cut pile.*

Saxony: *A variation of plush that has a bit more twist in the fibers, making them stand up straight and show fewer footprints.*

Whatever texture you choose, insist on density. In general, the denser the carpet, the longer it will last. That's because, in a dense carpet, the individual fibers are packed so close together that they support one another. Basically, you walk only on the tips of the fiber tufts. If the pile is sparse, the yarn folds over and you expose more of each individual fiber to wear and tear.

So how are you supposed to tell how dense a carpet is? One way is to bend a piece of the carpet backward. If a lot of backing is visible through the pile, you need to up-grade to a higher quality. Another option: Ask the salesperson. Even though they aren't eager to reveal the secret, the industry has precise measurements of density. Grab the salesperson by the sleeve and ask about the "face weight" of each of the brands you're considering.

Key Lingo

*The **face weight** is the number of ounces of pile yarn in a square yard of carpet; it takes into account the number of tufts per square inch, plus the height of the pile. The higher the number, the denser the carpet; the denser the carpet, the better.*

Behind the scenes. Don't assume that the padding doesn't matter because it won't show. It pays to invest in good padding that will absorb shock and create a more comfortable surface underfoot. The price of most carpets includes installation and padding, but you might want to ask about options to upgrade the padding. If the difference is only a couple of dollars per square yard, it may be worth it —and it may actually increase the life of your carpet.

After pondering over the carpet fibers, you probably don't want to think much about the pads. So don't worry. Just use felted hair-and-jute padding—the sturdiest type— in high-traffic areas such as hallways and stairs, and settle on synthetics, such as the new urethane or shredded rebonded urethane pads, in the rest of the house. Even if you some-times feel you want padded floors and walls, don't let the padding get too thick. Too much padding can cause the carpet to bend and flex, causing premature wear and stretching. Stick to pads $^3/_8$ to $^1/_2$ inch thick. No more, no less.

The stain pain. If you walk on it, your carpet is going to get dirty and probably stained. The amount of discoloration depends on the type of yarn, the source of the stain, and how quickly you clean up any messes.

Think of a strand of yarn as either a carrot or radish. Some solution-dyed carpets contain fibers that are colored when the yarn is made, so the color goes through the entire fiber ("a carrot"); other fibers are dyed afterward, so the color coats but does not penetrate the fiber ("a radish"). Carrots are far more stain-resistant than radishes because there are fewer so-called dye sites on the fibers to accept the spot.

Of course, there are trade-offs. Solution-dyed carpets are made of industrial-strength olefins and nylons; they have certain characteristics that might not make them your first choice for the interior of your home. Luckily, even yarn-dyed carpets usually come treated for additional stain resistance.

Before coating your carpet with Scotchguard or some other do-it-yourself antistaining treatment, check your warranty. Most carpets come with their own fiber treatment, as well as warranties from the carpet manufacturer and the fiber company. You probably don't need to do anything to the carpet for several years except clean it.

If you have your carpet cleaned and the professional cleaner tries to sell you a special treatment, resist the temptation (and hard sell). You won't need additional treatments until your existing warranty expires. Some silicone-based treatments can actually cause rapid soiling, since the dirt can stick to the silicone. Beware: Some treatments can actually void a manufacturer's warranty. Play it safe and check your warranty; most manufacturers try to make it easy on you by providing a toll-free consumer hotline.

In search of the perfect fit. Wall-to-wall carpet should be installed by a pro who knows how to stretch it to fit without bulges or bumps. Any carpet will stretch some after it's put down, so you want to make sure it's as taut as possible at the beginning. Some carpets, especially cheap ones, tend to stretch more than others. Before buying a carpet, ask whether the dealer will pay to have the carpet restretched if it starts to look slack in six months.

Ready for action. While you're at it, find out what condition the room needs to be in when the installer arrives. You may have to pay a little extra if you want someone else to pick up the old carpet and haul it away. Likewise, you may be able to get help moving furniture—but it may cost an additional fee.

Don't Forget to Ask

- ☐ *Will the color fade under the light conditions in my room?*
- ☐ *Does the price include installation and padding?*
- ☐ *Will I have to pay extra to have furniture moved?*
- ☐ *Will I have to pay extra to have the old carpet picked up and hauled away?*
- ☐ *Is there an extra charge for installing on stairs?*
- ☐ *In six months, if the carpet needs to be restretched, who will have to pay for the service?*

Chapter Two

COMPUTERLAND
QUICKSAND

■ CompuSecrets: What the Dealer Doesn't Tell You

Spending a lot of money is no guarantee that a personal computer will make your life any easier. It takes a lot of commitment to figure out what kind of system you need, and then a lot of time to figure out where to get it for a fair price and with the right service.

Before you get lost in cyberspace, ask yourself these questions:

What do you plan to do with the machine? Before you decide what kind of computer you need, you have to determine what kind of software you want to use on it. The basic types of uses are wordprocessing, spreadsheets, graphics, and games. Of course, your needs will probably evolve during the time you have the machine, but it's a good idea to think about what you *expect* to do with the computer before you shop.

Do you want an Apple or an IBM system? Alas, there are no shortcuts to making this important decision. The Apple systems tend to be easier to use, but they are slower and less flexible. More important, considerably less software is available for the Apple than the IBM (which includes so-called clones).

Before deciding on which type of system, consider what kind of machine you use at work and, if you plan to swap disks back and forth, what machines your friends use at home. Your life will be easier if you can avoid translating files from one system to the other. Sure, it's possible, but often some material is lost in the translation.

Windows software allows you to get the best of both worlds. With Windows installed on an IBM machine, you can use a mouse and follow the same easy-to-read graphic commands as those used with Apple computers. Windows performs at its best when running Windows-specific programs, such as Word for Windows or Wordperfect for Windows. It can also run other software programs written for IBM computers, but the graphics won't be quite as nifty.

What type of machine? Now comes the tough part. You'll have lots of choices to make—some easy, some not so easy.

■ **Speed of processor:** Think of a computer like a car —the more you spend, the faster it goes. As a novice, you'll probably want to consider the 486 machine. (Don't even look at the 386 models—they cost almost as much and they're five to ten times slower.) There are two basic model lines: SX and DX. The SX is basically a cheaper, slower version that costs about $150 less.

■ **Amount of RAM (Random Access Memory):** This is the brain capacity of your computer while it's thinking. The more RAM, the faster the machine. Don't go below 4 RAM, 8 is better. Make sure you can add additional RAM, bringing the total up to 16 RAM. In general, get more than you need today; software isn't getting any less complex.

■ **Hard-drive space:** This is like the long-term memory of your computer's brain. You want to be sure the computer has enough hard-drive space to store all your software and documents. A good starting point would be 340 megabytes, which will cost about $100

more than a 120 megabyte basic machine. You'll
need even more—as much as 500 to 600 megabytes
—if you want to use graphics or sophisticated
games.

■ **Video card and monitor:** This will determine what
the screen you're working on looks like. Make sure
it's easy on the eyes: With a monochrome (one
color), go with the green; it's easier to look at than
black (amber comes in second). Better yet, choose a
color monitor; current models can display as many
as 16.7 million colors, depending on the power and
sophistication of the video inside your computer.

Whether color or monochrome, buy the monitor with the highest resolution (greatest number of
dots per inch) you can afford. The images are made
up of tiny little dots; the more dots, the clearer
the picture, and the easier to read for extended
periods.

■ **The extras:** You'll be confronted with a number of
add-ons, such as:

• A _modem_ allows your computer to communicate
over the phone lines. You can pick one up for as
little as $50. If you're interested, buy one when
you get the computer so that you won't have to
deal with any problems about compatibility. For
about $100 you can get a modem that also works
as a fax machine, allowing you to send or receive
documents stored in your computer by fax.

• _CD-ROMs_ (Read Only Memory) allow your computer to read information from compact discs just
like those used to play music. The CD fits into a
slot in your computer (just like the slot for a
floppy disk). Vast amounts of information can be
stored on a CD. For example, CDs are encoded
with an entire encyclopedia, or phone books from

across the country. Anyone buying a computer today should spend the necessary $200 to $400 and get a CD-ROM.

I'm running just as fast as I can. As a general rule, buy the fastest, most powerful machine you can afford rather than the cheapest you can get by with. For the additional money, you'll get extra memory or a faster chip, which can be used to operate newer, easier, and more exciting software programs. You may even save money in the long run because you may use the more powerful system longer before you "outgrow" it.

Keep it legal. Many computers come with preloaded software to run the operating system, and some even come with application software, such as a wordprocessing or spreadsheet program. Be sure that any preloaded software is properly licensed by the software manufacturer. Be sure you get all the manuals and paperwork. When you get home, call the software manufacturer and double check to make sure you have a legitimate copy of the software. If you don't, if you run into trouble, the software manufacturer won't provide any assistance.

That's Bull

While advertisers may claim a computer is 100 percent compatible, don't assume that a "clone" can do everything the original machine can do. In some cases the machines are software compatible but not hardware compatible. You must also be wary of "brand name" machines. Sometimes the machines will only accept "brand name" keyboards, monitors, and other add-ons, which may be more expensive than their no-name counterparts. Before you buy, find out whether your computer, monitor, and keyboard all speak the same language.

Can't you understand English? Always read the manual before buying software. If the instructions are incomprehensible, then the software may not be clear either. Scrap it and choose a program you can understand. Life is challenging enough without allowing an inanimate object to make you feel stupid.

Do you feel the electricity between us? You may not feel it or even be aware that it's there, but the electricity coming out of most wall sockets doesn't come in a steady, even rate. The amount of energy varies with the demand, making power surges or spikes strong enough to damage delicate electronic equipment not only possible but likely. These surges can cause your screen to freeze, go blank, or worse—it can actually "fry" a computer's circuitry. To protect your machine, buy a voltage regulator or surge protector designed for computers and electronics gear. They cost about $20 and plug into the wall outlet; often they prove extra handy because they allow you to plug more than one device into the outlet.

One strike and you're out. When you're dealing with a lightning storm, a direct hit to the powerline can destroy a computer. When a lightning storm arrives, unplug the computer from the wall socket and your modem from the phone line—just to be safe.

Getting settled into your new home. When you buy a new computer, be sure to allow it to "burn in" by leaving the computer running (but the monitor off) for the first two weeks. During this trial period, any electric problems should show up, and the machine will still be under warranty. Some experts even suggest that fully 80 percent of the electrical circuits that survive a burn-in will last as long as five hundred years.

We're all the same beneath the skin. And so are most floppy disks. Most of the "magnetic media" are made by a few manufacturers and sold under a wide range of brand names. Shop by price, not by brand name.

You have the fingers of a pianist. But how about a keyboardist? Choose a keyboard that resembles a conventional electric typewriter keyboard with the QWERTY placement. Don't even consider models with flat compact keys that are hard to operate; you'll hate yourself for buying one because you'll spend half your time correcting typos. Try a few different keyboards to decide which feels right.

Key Lingo

Bit: *A tiny switch inside the computer that forms the nuts and bolts of all information storage.*

Boot: *To turn on the computer. To reboot is to reset.*

Byte: *Eight bits clumped together to form a single nugget of information (a character) inside the computer.*

CD-ROM: *Compact Disc—Read Only Memory. An optical storage disk containing millions of bytes of information.*

CPU: *Central Processing Unit. A term for the computer's microprocessor or brain.*

DOS: *Disk Operating System. The program that controls the machine, the programs that run on it.*

Hard disk: *A long-term storage file inside the computer. They are faster and hold more than floppy disks.*

Megabyte: *One million bytes. That's a lot. War and Peace could fit into a megabyte, no problem.*

Modem: *Stands for modulator-demodulator, a device that translates electronic information in the computer to sounds that can be transmitted over phone lines.*

The myth of the Retail Price. How much should you pay for a computer? Don't rely on the manufacturer's suggested retail price for guidance; this figure has almost no basis in fact. The so-called street price can be 40 percent lower, especially if you're willing to shop by mail. For your first computer, it probably makes sense to shop at a retail store; you'll pay more, but you should get the additional support you need.

I wanna hold your hand. Sometimes we all need a little help from our friends at the computer store. Before buying from a retail outlet, check out the amount and quality of the technical service. Some direct marketers offer free technical support over the phone via a toll-free number. Some local merchants offer on-site service contracts for a flat fee; some even include this as part of the warranty and fold the cost into the price of the machine. In any case, find out how much help you're going to get before you get in over your head.

■ NO MORE "I CAN'T READ YOUR WRITING": PICKING A BLACK-AND-WHITE PRINTER

For most computer users, a printer isn't a luxury but a necessity. After all, once you have used the computer to process information or write a document, you're going to want to put it on paper. How that document looks depends on the kind of printer you choose.

Connect the dots. We're all familiar with the tried-and-true dot-matrix printers, which are still the only game in town at the low-cost end of the market. These printers offer decent appearance with moderate speed at a low price, and they even print graphics. Dot-matrix printers work by activating a cluster of tiny pins that strike different patterns on a print ribbon. These prints aren't quiet as they go about their work; printing involves a lot of loud buzzing and whines as the print head scrambles back and forth across the page. If you can stand the noise, dot-matrix printers offer a real value for the money; 9-pin printers go for less than $200; more refined 24-pin models typically run $100 to $300 more. Unless you're going to be printing draft-quality text only, spend the money and go for the 24-pin model; the text looks better and the machines often handle more variations in typefaces or fonts.

Don't even think about parking that printer here. Don't waste time looking at daisy-wheel impact printers. These outdated printers work like an electronic typewriter, with a spinning "golf ball" wheel that strikes the paper. This used to be the only way to get decent letter-quality printing, so people put up with the head-splitting noise, the slow pace, and the absolute lack of graphics options. Nowadays you've got choices. Cross the daisy-wheel off your shopping list.

An octopus couldn't have said it any better. Now that you've eliminated daisy-wheel printers from consideration, inkjet printers become the next step up from dot-matrix printers. Inkjet models work much the same as dot-matrix printers do, except that instead of striking a ribbon, the pins shoot tiny drops of ink onto the paper. They are much faster and quieter than dot-matrix printers, and at about $500, their price falls between the 24-pin dot-matrix printer and the less-expensive laser printers.

Laser surgery on your text. Laser printers offer top-of-the-line print quality, just like from a typesetter. The machines have virtually unlimited graphic capability, they can print three to seventeen pages a minute, and they're almost silent. The downside, of course, is cost: close to $1,000 for a basic model. Your text will look lovely, but you may find yourself spending more money on the printer than on the computer.

Feed your printer a well-balanced diet. When

your printer is hungry, you have several paper options, depending on the type of printer you settle on. Many dot-matrix printers allow you to choose either single sheets or continuous-feed (track-fed) paper, which has vertical holes on the sides of the paper to pull it through. Continuous-feed paper usually comes in standard white, green-and-white striped, and business quality.

Laser printers have delicate stomachs. They rely on an electrical charge to hold the toner to the paper, and then heat and pressure to fuse the toner to the page. Good laser paper will have special electrical- and heat-resistance properties, just as copy-machine paper does. Buy the good stuff made for laser printers and copy machines; it's less likely to curl, jam, and give you headaches. In addition, cheap papers can leave lots of lint inside your printer, compromising print quality and shortening engine life. With an inkjet printer, you'll need to buy heavy paper (24-pound) to avoid unsightly bleed-through.

Don't Forget to Ask

☐ *What kind of paper do I need?*
☐ *How fast will this machine print?*
☐ *How many different fonts or typefaces can it print?*
☐ *Can I add additional fonts?*
☐ *How much noise does the machine make?*
☐ *Are my printer and computer compatible?*
☐ *Can the printer accommodate envelopes? Odd-sized papers?*
☐ *Can the printer do "landscape" or sideways printing?*

I'm meltinnnnng . . . If you're going to use your laser printer to print labels, buy the special labels designed for laser printers, even if they cost more. The roller inside a laser printer can exceed a scorching 200 degrees, too hot for the adhesive on some cheaper labels made for impact printers. Unless you want melted adhesive glopping up the inside of your printer, buy the labels recommended for your machine. For the same reason, don't run raised-ink printing or embossed stationery through your laser printer.

■ JUST THE FAX, MA'AM

After about twenty seconds of high-pitched whines and shrill cries, a fax machine "shakes hands" with its partner and begins to send or receive an image. Ah, the miracle of high-tech wizardry. While all these machines deserve our awe and respect, when it comes to buying a fax machine, some are considerably handier than others.

You can pick up a basic fax machine for home use for $300 to $600, depending on the features you choose. The less expensive models typically omit automatic paper cutters and document feeders, two useful features. If you don't want to deal with thermal fax paper, you can opt for a plain-paper machine that consumes regular bond paper, but it'll cost you. Plain paper machines cost $750 _and up._

These days, almost all fax machines have a switch that allows the fax machine to share a line with your regular voice phone line. (In the old days, you had to spend $15 or $20 a month for a designated phone line for the fax machine.) Today's fax machines also allow you to connect them directly to an answering machine so that you won't miss any phone messages if you're out.

Hello. Hello? Hello! If your fax machine does share a line with your regular telephone and you answer a call, only to hear the warbling and squeals of another fax machine in dialogue, you want to be able to tell the machine that you're sorry for interrupting and to please accept the fax. Look for a machine that allows you to start the machine from an extension phone by hitting the "*" key on the telephone pad or by hitting the "start" button on the machine itself.

Slow down; I'm thinking. Speedy machines can send a page of single-spaced typed text in about a minute; photographs using the halftone (or the ultra-fine setting) take about five minutes on average. Don't settle for a slow machine unless you plan to use it only to order from catalogs and pass notes to your friends. You'll go nuts waiting as you send long documents—and you'll face higher phone bills if you send long-distance faxes.

A cut above. Don't even consider a machine that doesn't have an automatic paper cutter. Sure, you might save a couple of hundred dollars by investing in a new pair of scissors instead of a machine with a paper cutter, but you'll hate yourself. You don't want to go nuts flattening the scroll that will eventually be your ten-page document. Indulge, you're worth it.

Feed me! Feed me! Unless you long for the days of spoon-feeding your toddler and know that you will find satisfaction in feeding your hungry machine one page at a time, go for a fax with an automatic document feeder. Look for a model that can gobble down ten to twenty pages in a sitting.

Give it to me straight. Thermal or plain paper? That is the question. And the answer depends on how much money you want to spend—plain paper copiers cost about twice as much as their thermal-paper kin. No doubt about it, plain paper is much nicer to work with; thermal paper curls and tends to fade over time when exposed to light. (Beware the slow fade: Photocopy any document on thermal paper if you want to keep it for posterity's sake.) Machines with anticurl systems work pretty well, but you'll still need to make copies to avoid fading.

Trivia to Impress Your Friends

One of every four calls placed on U.S. phone lines carries a fax message, not a voice.

That's Bull

Some people will try to sell you on the idea that a fax machine connected to your computer via a modem is just as good as a separate fax machine. True, computers with faxing ability, either because they came with a fax system or because about $100 or more of extra hardware and software has been added, can be easy to use, but they're not without drawbacks. Computer faxes allow you to fax documents stored in your computer, but they don't let you send newspaper articles, drawings, and other items not in your computer. Further, you can only receive faxes when the machine is turned on, so if you get messages in the wee hours of the morning—or any time your computer wouldn't be turned on—then a traditional fax may be best for you.

Don't Forget to Ask

Don't count on the counsel of the guy behind the counter when it comes to buying a fax machine. Instead, before heading for the business supply store, ask yourself the following questions:

☐ *How fast a machine do I need?*

☐ *Do I need a plain-paper machine?*

☐ *How crowded will my desktop be with yet another office device?*

☐ *What add-on features and gadgets are important to me?*

■ ON CALL: SELECTING A CELLULAR PHONE

A generation ago, callers used to be more patient. No answer? No problem, just try again later. Away from home or the office? Sit tight, and use the phone when you get back. Face it: Those days are gone. Enter the communications era, complete with cellular phones that allow you to send and receive calls from your car, your briefcase, or even the handset tucked in your pocket or purse.

A phone for every appetite. There are several types of cellular phones, depending on just how much you fear falling out of touch.

- A *mobile or car phone* draws its power from the car's battery. This phone consists of an antenna mounted on the roof of the car, a handset installed inside the car, and a transmitter stored inside the trunk.
- A *transportable or "bag" phone* contains the same components, only they're housed together (along with a

separate battery pack) in a purselike bag that weighs about five pounds. These phones don't work very well inside cars because the antenna is inside the car.

- A *portable cellular phone* includes the same basic components in a single handset weighing less than a pound. Some portables have more limited power, which can create problems in areas with poor service, but the problem can be overcome by buying a kit that boosts the transmitter power to 3 watts, the same as the other types.

By the way, the dial tone is extra. You can buy a phone as a status symbol for the interior of your car, but if you want to use it, you'll have to pay for the privilege. Buying a phone is only half the battle; you also need to select one of the two cellular phone companies that serve your area. Most companies try to sell you the service when you're shopping for the phone. Cheap phone-purchase deals often have expensive service contracts and high rates for calls, so be sure to look at your total cost. More so than with many other products, it pays to shop around for the best phone-and-service deal, taking into account differences in the monthly charges. The exact same model phone can vary by hundreds of dollars from store to store. Some companies even give away the phones, provided the customer signs an extended contract for service.

It's healthy to avoid long-term commitments. At least those between you and your cellular phone company. Until you test the service and know it meets your needs, make the shortest-term commitment you can. If you sign up for one year of service and decide to cancel, you can face penalties of several hundred dollars. Date around before getting engaged.

A chain is as strong as its weakest link. And a cellular system is only as powerful as its weakest cell. When a call is placed, it is fed through a network of low-power

That's Bull

Some lazy dealers may tell you that a roof-mount antenna can be used on the trunk. Don't listen. Antennas are designed for a specific mounting location, even though some lazy dealers would rather cut corners and slap a roof antenna on the trunk than go to the trouble of working the cable underneath the interior molding of the car to reach to the antenna base mounted on the roof. A roof antenna belongs on the roof. If you accept sloppy work from the installer, you'll have to settle for sloppy reception from the phone.

transmission stations (the cells). Your call is handed off from cell to cell as you drive along. Normally, you won't know when you've moved into a new cell; however, if there is no available channel for your call in the new cell, then your call will be abruptly dropped. No "see you later," no "bye-bye." You want a company that provides strong service throughout your calling area.

Talk is cheap. Unless you're on a cellular phone. The cost of calls mounts quickly, since you're billed for both incoming and outgoing calls. You'll have to check into the various service plans offered by the companies in your area, but most provide an economy service ($20 or $30 monthly fee and you pay by the minute for calls), a basic plan (a higher monthly fee with thirty minutes or so of "free" calls), and an executive plan ($100 or $200 monthly fee with several hours of airtime, making the per-minute cost significantly lower). If you're not sure how much you'll use the phone, start with the least expensive plan and see if you can live with it. You may be able to get on a corporate plan through your business, which can save money.

More Bull

Some dealers will promise a certain rate, say $39 for 30 minutes of calling. What they conveniently forget to mention is that the rate applies only in certain limited calling areas. Make sure you know the exact terms before signing on the dotted line.

There's power in numbers. When you're away from the office, you're away from your phone directory—but not with many models of cellular phones that allow you to program more than forty speed-dial numbers. No, you don't have to memorize forty access codes. Virtually all of the phones have a display that tells you the number you are dialing; when looking for a programmed phone number, some phones will print out the name of the person you're calling as you scroll through the list. This is a nice little extra, especially since your address book and Rolodex probably won't be sitting in the front seat next to you.

Look ma, no hands. It's one thing to ride a two-wheeler with your hands off the handlebars and quite another to drive a four-wheeler with your hands on the phone instead of the steering wheel. Choose a model with a speaker-phone option so that you can talk without holding the handset. Granted, the sound quality isn't great (is that a tin can you're driving?), but safety first.

Don't call us, we'll call you. That's what you're telling your callers when you block all calls to your phone. This optional feature can save money in unwanted calls, and it can give you the much-needed ability to return to that blissful state of "incommunicado."

It (still) isn't polite to eavesdrop. But people do it all the time. Because you're using airwaves to place your call, anyone with a radio scanner that receives cellular frequencies can listen in if you're using a cellular or portable phone. Congress threw a wet blanket over eavesdropping hobbyists by banning the manufacture of scanners that pick up cellular frequencies, but enough units have already been sold that you should be aware of the potential breach of privacy before airing your dirty laundry over the airwaves.

Don't Forget to Ask

Before buying a cellular car phone, ask your insurance agent if you need to change your auto insurance policy. Most companies don't cover theft, unless you buy additional coverage at a cost of about $50 a year.

If you're concerned about the unauthorized use of your phone, ask your service provider for an access code or personal identification number. You'll have to punch in a few more numbers before placing a call, but you'll enjoy more security in knowing your phone won't be used without your permission.

■ EASY ANSWERS: PICKING AN ANSWERING MACHINE

Time was if you called someone who wasn't at home, the telephone rang and rang until you got tired of waiting and hung up. Nowadays, you're expected to "leave a message at the tone" so that the person you are calling can "get back to you as soon as possible." Answering machines can be an annoyance or a lifesaver, depending on whether you're

ultimately able to reach out and actually touch someone—
and whether or not your answering machine works properly.

Sure, there are times when you want to use the excuse
that your answering machine "ate" the message and that's
why you didn't return a call, but you want to use this feeble
defense at your discretion, not because your machine really
did garble a message. Luckily, the latest generation of answering devices have a pretty good track record compared
to earlier models. Though you may have to accept a few lost
messages once in a while, most machines get the messages
straight.

There are three main types of machines: single-cassette
models, dual-cassette models, and microchip models:

- _Single-cassette machines_ are the old-fashioned type that
  use one audio cassette to record both the outgoing
  message and the callers' messages. You can pick up
  one of these bottom-of-the-line machines for about
  $40. They answer calls just fine, but your callers will
  have to endure a relatively long pause as the machine
  advances the tape to the appropriate space to record
  the message.
- _Dual-cassette machines_ work much the same way as
  their single-cassette cousins, except that these machines have separate tapes for outgoing and incoming
  messages, so callers won't have to wait long to begin
  speaking. These machines start at about $50 or so.
  They use either mini-cassettes or full-sized tapes.
  The choice is yours: The mini-cassette machines take
  up less desk space; the full-size machines use regular
  audio tapes.
- _Microchip machines_ use digital memory chips to record
  messages. Some models get quite high tech—and
  expensive. For $150 or so you can get a machine
  that doesn't use audio tapes, recording the messages

on an internal chip instead. Some sophisticated models, which can cost up to $300, have "mailboxes" so that callers can direct calls to specific family members.

Machines that use digital memory chips don't leave much time for messages. For example, a machine with a memory chip might limit the outgoing message to thirty seconds and the incoming messages to one minute. Warn your less than fast-talking friends to collect their thoughts so that they aren't cut off mid-senten . . .

Yes, but does it know shorthand? Top-notch machines don't stop with simply answering the phone and recording messages. Oh no, these devices do all the work of an entire secretarial pool. Many have built-in phones, either standard or cordless. They can tell you the date and time of the call; they can answer multiple phone lines with multiple messages; some even allow you to eavesdrop on the room by activating a room-monitor function. Of course, the more gadgets you want, the more you can expect to pay. Fancy models with all the extras can run $200 to $300 or more— and they don't take coffee breaks.

On the line. If you have more than one telephone line, you can choose a single machine to field calls from two separate numbers. Both dual-cassette and microchip machines can recognize the distinctive rings and keep the messages straight—for a price. Two-line machines typically cost about $200 for a dual-cassette model or $300 for a microchip system.

Get the message? All answering machines sold today allow you to call the machine and find out if you received any calls by using a remote access code. Most machines also have a "toll saver" feature—your phone rings a set number of times before the answering machine picks up if you have a message and a shorter number of rings if you don't. For example, if you call your machine long-distance, it might ring twice and then begin to recite your messages, but if it rings three or four times, you know that no one has called, so you can hang up before facing any long-distance charges.

Don't test your callers' patience. Some machines allow you to record long, rambling introductory messages. Spare your friends; don't do it. Even if your oh-so-clever greeting amuses callers the first time they hear it, you'll find that even your closest friends will hang up rather than endure listening to it after a while. Do everyone a favor and keep the message short and sweet.

The Voice Mail Alternative

Next time you call a friend, you may hear the same annoying automated voice that you're forced to endure when you call most business establishments. "Voice mail" has gone suburban.

A number of phone companies now allow residential households to sign up for full-blown voice-mail service. The system answers calls, records messages, and sends the recordings to as many as eight different electronic "mailboxes," one for every member of the household. The system also transfers callers into the voice-mail system if someone calls and the line is busy.

If you have a call in your mailbox, the dial tone stutters, indicating that there's a message waiting for you. Using a Touch-Tone phone, you can retrieve the message by punching in a code. Voice mail is a reliable and efficient system for many households, but it's pricey at $5 to $10 a month. At those rates, you could pay for the average answering machine in less than a year.

Don't Forget to Ask

☐ *How long do I have to record the outgoing message?*

☐ *How long do callers have to record incoming messages?*

☐ *Can I change my outgoing message? Can I do this when I'm away from home?*

☐ *Can I access messages when I'm away from home?*

☐ *Does the machine give the date and time of the call?*

☐ *Can the machine handle multiple phone lines?*

☐ *Does the machine provide "mailboxes" for family members to keep messages private?*

Chapter Three

MONEY MATTERS

■ EASY MONEY:
SENDING EMERGENCY CASH

You know the scene: The struggling college student needs extra cash or your best friend is out of town and gets a ticket for speeding—somebody is in trouble and needs you to send money *fast*. So what are your choices?

Before dialing the number of the organization whose advertising jingle is echoing in your brain, take a minute to consider your options. The four most common ways to send money are Western Union, American Express, bank wire transfers, and postal service money orders.

- *Western Union* allows you to dial "M" for Money by calling in a transaction by telephone and charging it to VISA or MasterCard. Of course, you can also visit a Western Union office and hand over the cash or cashier's check in person. At the other end of the transaction, the recipient is asked to show identification to prove the money is his or hers for the taking. What, no ID? You say your wallet was stolen? No problem. Western Union will simply ask one or two identifying questions (such as the tried and true: What is your mother's maiden name?) to affirm the recipient's identity. The entire process can take as little as ten minutes; as soon as the money is entered in the computer, the cash is available for pickup at any Western Union outlet, including a number of grocery stores and convenience stores.

- *American Express* provides much the same service, but you have to go into the office to initiate the transfer. Again, you give American Express the cash and, voila!, the cash or traveler's checks are available for your friend to pick up almost anywhere in the world.
- *Bank wire transfers* involve a bit more hassle. To wire money, you must have the code number assigned to the bank where you want the funds deposited. Don't know the number? Surely the courteous and helpful staff members at your local bank will be eager to help you track it down. This method won't work well for the typical emergency; if the timing is off it can take several days for the money to become available. (The money is credited for the next business day, but if you have to work around banking hours, weekends, and all those bank holidays, it could take two or three days.) The cost: a flat fee of about $10.
- *Postal service money orders,* as well as certified or cashier's checks, can also be used, but your recipient will have to wait for the little slip of paper to arrive in the mail. Just tell your friend, "The check is in the mail."

So why don't I do all my banking this way? Because you'd go broke paying the service fees. Emergencies are expensive: The two major services charge varying fees, depending on where you send the money and how much you send. For example, it can cost $29 to send $200, or up to $500 to send $10,000. Go ahead and make a quick call to both Western Union and American Express and find out how much your specific transaction would cost. Don't rely on reputation or advertising alone: One company may be cheaper for low amounts and another for higher sums.

■ THANKS FOR YOUR SUPPORT: DONATING TO CHARITIES WISELY

A number of worthwhile organizations depend on charitable contributions to do their good works, but it's not always easy to know where to give. Uncharitable charities can exploit the generosity of others by pocketing the donations or channeling a disproportionate amount of the money into fund-raising operations. Unless you want to give to the Fund-raisers Employment Fund, check out the charity before you write a check.

Generous to a fault. Though many donors assume that most of the money they give will go to the stated cause, there are no federal guidelines specifying how the money donated to charity must be spent. Though it might seem like fraud, charitable solicitations are protected by the First Amendment right to free speech, even when ninety-nine cents out of every dollar goes into fund-raising. To help you figure out when it makes sense to give, the Council of Better Business Bureaus in Arlington, Virginia, and the National Charities Information Bureau in New York City provide ratings or performance evaluations on a number of leading charitable organizations.

Keep the change. If you get a nice warm feeling every time you put a quarter in the honor box and pick up a piece of hard candy, here's some information that may give you a chill: The money often goes to the marketers who set up the boxes, not to the charity. In these situations, the charity may rent their name to the marketing outfit for a fixed amount of money, and the marketers get to pocket whatever cash is donated. The charity gets a token donation, but it won't collect all of the money you give. One exception: Most of the board displays with coin slots are owned by the charities named on them.

I gave at the office. Or better yet, I already gave directly. If you'd like to donate to a charity, consider making a donation directly to the organization rather than through a fund-raising group. You'll know the money went right to the charity, without any commission or cut going to the fund-raiser.

Have you got change for a $20? Don't let these words ever come out of your mouth when speaking to someone collecting door-to-door for a charitable organization. *Never* give cash. If you choose to make a donation, write a check, even if it's just for $5 or $10. Of course, make the check out to the organization, not the person collecting the money. It's the only way you can be sure the money gets to the charity. (The charity will send you a written confirmation of your donation, which allows you to claim a deduction on your federal income taxes.)

Don't even bother feeling guilty. Some charities will send calendars, greeting cards, and other gifts in an attempt to coerce you into making a donation. Federal law prohibits retailers from sending unordered merchandise, so you're free to assume these items are gifts. You're under no obligation to give a dime, and you can do so with a clear conscience.

Just leave me alone. Charities, like other direct marketing operations, sell or trade the names of their donors. Give to one group and you may start getting bombarded with hands-out letters from other groups. You can request that the group not rent, trade, or sell your name; do so by writing a separate letter to the executive director of the organization. If you don't, before long you'll be getting solicitations constantly as different groups trade your name back and forth.

Good cause, bad move. Some charities invite you to provide your credit card number so that a fixed sum can be charged to your account every month. This technique, which is particularly popular among save-a-child charities, isn't necessarily a bad idea, but you should exercise extreme caution when providing credit card information—to anyone.

There is no copyright on the disease. Or on the words National or American. Be careful when making a donation that you're giving to the organization you're thinking of. A lot of groups choose a knock-off name, one that many people will mistakenly assume belongs to another well-respected group. Proceed with caution.

Warning Signs

Unless you know what to look for, it's easy to fall prey to swindlers masquerading as do-gooders. These high-pressure tactics are often signs that you're dealing with a con artist with uncharitable intentions:

- *The group offers to send a messenger to your home to pick up a check. They may be trying to avoid the postal service— and charges of postal fraud.*

- *Someone calls on behalf of a charity and says, "I'm calling for" the charity, rather than "I'm calling from . . ." A subtle difference, yes, but it can be an indication that a telemarketing firm is collecting for a charity, and that means the collection agency is going to pocket a hefty portion of your contribution.*

- *A caller cites a recent tragedy or natural disaster and encourages you to provide financial information over the phone. Always ask for information in writing, then send your check directly to the charity involved. The needy people will still appreciate your donation a week from now.*

Don't Forget to Ask

☐ *Are you a paid solicitor? If not, are you a volunteer or a paid staff member?*

☐ *What percentage of the money will go to support the cause and how much to fund-raising?*

☐ *Specifically, what has the charitable organization done in the last three years to support the cause?*

☐ *Specifically, what does the charity plan to do in the next three years to support the cause?*

☐ *May I have some information in writing? (Fraudulent outfits won't have printed materials available in most cases.)*

■ CHECK IT OUT:
CHOOSING THE RIGHT
CHECKING ACCOUNT

In days gone by, banks provided the same, plain basic checking accounts to all their customers. But bank deregulation allowed banks to offer different accounts to different customers, depending on the size of their account balances. Once again, the rich get richer and the poor get poorer. In general, the lower your deposits, the higher your fees. People with large balances may even make money by putting their money in interest-bearing checking accounts.

There are three basic types of checking accounts:

- *Regular* checking accounts, which pay no interest,
- *NOW* checking accounts, which pay a fixed rate of interest that varies with the minimum balance, and
- *Super NOW* checking accounts, which pay "market-

rate'' interest levels depending on the account balance, but require higher minimum balances.
Don't assume that one type of account is necessarily better
than another. To find the best deal, you'll need to compare
the costs of doing business with each type of account. Sorry,
no shortcuts.

It pays to save. If you have enough money on deposit
to open an interest-bearing checking account without incur-
ring fees, do it. A recent federal banking law now requires
banks and savings institutions to tell you exactly what rate
of interest they pay. Sounds straightforward, but in the past
they hid behind different methods of calculating interest
that camouflaged the actual earnings. When comparing any
accounts that earn interest, compare the annual percentage
yield, which is the bottom line of how much interest you'll
earn during the year. Even after you open an account, continue to compare rates, since banks change their terms as
their needs for deposits change.

No more rubber checks. A number of banks offer
overdraft protection so that you can avoid bounced check
charges and humiliation by obtaining an overdraft credit line.
If you don't balance your checkbook in time to catch an
error that throws your account out of whack and you write
a bad check, the bank will cover it. Of course, you'll be
charged interest on the outstanding balance—often as much
as 18 percent until the money is repaid.

What a difference a day makes. Before making a
deposit, withdrawal, or closing an account, take a look at a
calendar. Many banks compound interest on your account
monthly, but pay it quarterly. If you close the account before the interest income is credited to your account at the
end of the quarter, you may lose it. Likewise, check the
schedule before making a large withdrawal.

The check is in the mail. Or the order form for
the new checks is. While many account holders assume that
the cheapest and easiest way to reorder checks is to order

them from the bank, you can buy them for half or one-third the price from a number of check-printing mail-order companies. Check it out.

But that's not my John Hancock—my name isn't even John. If your checkbook is lost or stolen, you need to notify the bank as soon as possible. The bank may urge you to stop payment on the missing checks as a precaution, but you'll have to pay a stop-payment fee of $10 to $20 or so for each missing check. Don't do it. It's the bank's responsibility to make sure that the signature on the checks matches the signature on file. If the checks are fraudulently used and the bank doesn't catch it, that's the bank's problem, not yours.

Who is this Uncle Sam? Some banks give nondepositors a hard time about cashing checks, including those issued by the U.S. government. Check-cashing outlets that do accept the checks often charge exorbitant fees for the privilege. If you're ever in a situation where you need to cash a government check away from your home bank, compare rates carefully; in the past, some check-cashing outlets have charged as much as an unbelievable 20 percent to cash a government check.

All's clear. Federal banking regulations require that a bank clear a local check in one working day and all other checks within five business days. Before writing checks against money you just deposited, make sure the checks have cleared or you could face significant overdraft charges.

I'll give you the money, but it's going to cost you. Many banks nickel-and-dime their account holders by adding little fees for every little transaction. For example, you might be hit with a fee of 50 cents to make a withdrawal from the bank's automatic-teller machine, or $1 if the ATM belongs to another bank. Before choosing a bank, compare the costs of these small, cost-of-doing-business fees. They can add up—fast.

Don't Forget to Ask

☐ *Are you insured by the Federal Deposit Insurance Corporation? (If so, your account will be insured for up to $100,000 per account.)*

☐ *What are the fees to maintain the account?*

☐ *If the fees vary with the minimum balance, how is the balance calculated?*

☐ *Will the account earn interest? What is the annual yield?*

☐ *What is the charge for bouncing a check? Stopping payment on a check? Using an automatic-teller machine at the bank? Using an automatic-teller machine at another bank?*

☐ *What is the policy regarding overdraft protection?*

■ POWERFUL PLASTIC: PICKING A CREDIT CARD

The average American carries around a wallet stuffed with seven or eight charge cards. In this world of credit, there are most definitely winners and losers: The banks are the winners and the cardholders are split between both camps, depending on how smart they are about choosing and using their cards.

All plastic is not the same. Thousands of different banks and financial institutions issue credit cards bearing the MasterCard or VISA name, but the cardholder terms are as different as the banks issuing them. When debating the merits of different card offers, you should consider the following:

■ **The annual fee:** Most banks charge a flat annual fee

for the privilege of carrying a card. Fees are usually in the $15 to $50 range, though some banks waive the fee entirely, and others charge $250 or more, especially for the "premium" gold and platinum cards.

- **The grace period:** The time period during which you can pay off your bill in full without being subject to any interest payments or finance charges. Under most credit card agreements, if you don't pay the entire bill, all new purchases will accrue finance charges immediately. This grace period is usually at least twenty-five days, though a few banks have started luring consumers with low interest rates, then slapping them with interest from the date of purchase. A credit card without a grace period is no bargain. You can find a better deal.

- **The interest rate:** Look at the amount of interest you have to pay on your unpaid balances. If you pay your bill in full each month, then you won't have to worry much about the interest rate, and you can afford to look for an account with no annual fee, even if it carries a slightly higher interest rate.

- **The goodies:** Many credit cards offer bonuses—anything from free insurance on rental cars to bonus miles on a frequent-flier program. Watch the bottom line and you may find you're paying a stiff annual fee in order to collect those "free" miles or other benefits. Don't be lured by the extras alone: A good card needs to combine low fees, low interest, and a fair grace period. The extras are, after all, extra.

Pick a card, any card. Chances are the best offers won't come knocking at your mailbox. The most favorable card rates and terms are often offered by mid-size regional banks. You can apply for a credit card from any out-of-state bank, but you may need to hunt for the best deal. The

Bankcard Holders of America (524 Branch Drive, Salem, VA 24153; 703-389-5445) compiles lists of low-cost credit cards across the country.

Trivia to Impress Your Friends

Americans charge more than $300 billion on their credit cards each year, and pay about $35 billion in interest on those loans.

Timing is everything. If you're planning to make an expensive purchase, try to buy after the billing date so it won't show up until the following month's statement. By timing your purchases just right, you can get a "float" on your money (or an interest-free loan) for as much as fifty days.

Too much of a good thing. While getting credit and using it wisely is one way to establish a good credit rating, too much credit can actually undermine your credit-worthiness. The credit limits on all your accounts are included in your credit report. If you have a large number of credit cards—even if you have no history of delinquency and have never used the cards—they can interfere with a mortgage application or car loan because you *could* go out and run up bills on those cards. The moral: Close accounts that you don't need or use, including department store, gasoline, and extra bank credit cards. Also, don't allow creditors to increase your limits beyond what you really need. Sure, it's nice to know that you can spend $5,000 with nothing but your signature to back it up, but these inflated limits can come back to haunt you later.

Avoiding risky business. The credit card issuer's

job is to convince creditworthy people to borrow as much as possible. But there's more; the issuer must also pull the rug out from people who are in over their heads and won't be able to pay. As part of the balancing act, card issuers routinely reevaluate card holders to find out if they're still acceptable risks. Warning signs of trouble include people who have spent up to the limit and make minimum payments, sometimes asking to increase the limit more and more. If the bank decides that you've got too much debt, it can unilaterally withdraw your card, leaving you with a whopping bill and no plastic.

Tell us a little bit about yourself. Well, I'm five feet, seven inches tall . . . No, no. The card issuer wants to know how long you've lived at your current address, whether you rent or own your home, how long you've been at your current job, and so forth. Most creditors have a complex formula they use to score credit applicants based on these and other factors. One way to increase the odds of being accepted is to avoid applying for other credit six months before applying for a credit card. Every inquiry into your file is noted in the report, and too many inquiries is grounds for automatic rejection.

A lesson from Economics 101. A number of credit card companies offer college students credit cards, even though they often have little or no income while they're in school. Though many students learn the lessons of mismanaging credit the hard way, getting a credit card can be easier when in school than when out in the cruel world. If you're capable of controlling your spending, it may be better to get a credit card while still in college than it will be as a graduate with a stable income and few credit references.

Make me an offer I can't refuse. In the highly competitive credit card market, you may be able to negotiate a lower rate on your existing cards. If you're a good customer and pay your bills on time, it can't hurt to call your credit card company and explain that you've received offers for cards with lower rates. You may be able to get the company to lower your interest rate without the hassle of closing one account and opening another.

"I'm not paying for that piece of junk." And you don't have to worry about trying to get your money back if you've paid with a credit card. If there's a problem with a purchase or if it's not delivered on time or if it doesn't meet your specifications, you can refuse to pay your credit card bill until the issue is resolved. Just be sure to follow the instructions of the card issuer by notifying them of the problem.

That's Bull

During the holiday season, many credit card issuers send their cardholders special notices offering to lower or even waive the monthly payment. Your friendly banker is really a Scrooge masquerading as Bob Cratchit. What often isn't pointed out (except, perhaps, in the small print) is that this generous offer doesn't waive the interest payment. In essence, you've been cordially invited to pay the bank more interest. Oh, by the way, happy holidays.

■ TO DIE FOR: BUYING LIFE INSURANCE

Most people have trouble thinking about death, especially their own. It's no wonder that most mortals dread the choices they must confront when buying life insurance. And the insurance companies don't make it any easier; the products they offer and the way they package them seem designed more to confuse than to enlighten.

In the universe of life insurance, there are two basic types of policies:

- *Term insurance,* which provides a stated amount of coverage to your heirs if you die during the period or term the policy is in force, and
- *Cash-value insurance,* which combines a death benefit and an investment plan; cash-value insurance is more expensive for the same amount of insurance protection.

Saving for a rainy day. Cash-value insurance is a long-term investment. People get into trouble, and lose a lot of money, by assuming that they can keep a policy in force for a couple of years, then cash it in. Though your insurance agent won't tell you during the sales pitch, cash-value policies usually make sense only if you keep them and make the payments for fifteen to twenty years. Most people can't withstand the long-term commitment; more than half the people who buy cash-value policies drop them within

That's Bull

Seeing isn't always believing. When an insurance agent gives you the spiel about cash-value policies, you'll see a series of graphs or so-called illustrations of what your investment could look like down the road. Of course, your actual investment will vary, depending on what happens to interest rates and the economy, but the salesperson may forget to mention that part. If the projections don't pan out, you may have to pay more in premiums or accept less insurance protection . . . surprise!

ten years, surrendering a disproportionate share of their money to the company.

A premium deal. The reason it takes so long for cash-value policies to get up to speed is that almost all of your first-year premium goes to the agent and his or her superiors. In the later years the percentage that goes into commission falls off, but not entirely.

Where there's smoke. Many insurance companies offer lower premiums to nonsmokers. If you can't kick the habit, don't compound your problem by trying to lie on your life insurance application about your smoking. A growing number of companies are using the required urine sample that's part of the physical to screen for traces of nicotine in addition to illegal drugs. The test doesn't give false positives for passive smokers, but it can detect people who have smoked within the last twenty-four to thirty-six hours. Most insurance companies won't tell you about the screening, unless, of course, you flunk the test.

Death-bed confession. In most cases, if someone lies about smoking and the insurance company later learns that the deceased was a smoker, the death benefit is still paid out, only the final amount is changed to reflect the amount of insurance the person could have purchased at the smokers' rate.

Squander your money on yourself. Don't give it to an insurance company. Forget buying cancer or other so-called dread-disease policies that insure against a single illness. These policies pay out very little in benefits, compared to the amount collected in premiums, making them a bad insurance value. Likewise, skip the policies for your children. Insurance is designed to protect dependents from financial hardship in case something happens to the breadwinner. Insure your child only if he or she is contributing to the support of the family.

Churning is for butter. But some greasy insurance

salesmen try to do it to unsuspecting policyholders. Once someone has stuck with a cash-value policy long enough that it's starting to show a meaningful return, some agents will urge you to switch to a new policy, theoretically to earn a higher yield, but in actuality so that the agent can collect that handsome commission all over again. In the biz, this practice is called "churning." To the rest of us, it's called "thievery."

Make me an offer I won't refuse. Some insurance companies offer low-load cash-value policies, but do everything they can not to let you know it. Low-load cash-value policies have significantly lower commissions because they are sold by telephone and by financial planners rather than by insurance agents. No agents, no agent's commission. It's that simple.

Advice Is Cheap

Don't rely on an insurance agent to tell you how much and what kind of life insurance you need. The agent is going to push the products that offer the best commissions, and often the agent will encourage you to buy more insurance than you need.

"Sure, cash-value policies are a little more expensive, but how can you afford not to provide the best plan for your family?"

"This is not just insurance, this is an investment."

"Isn't it better to provide a little bit too much protection than not enough?"

Overcoming the pitch takes a lot of strength—and research. Ultimately, it will be up to you to figure out what you need. Tedious though it may be, go to the library and check out a couple of books on insurance before talking to an agent. Unfortunately, there are no reliable shortcuts.

■ BUYING YOUR WAY IN: INVESTING IN A MUTUAL FUND

Mutual funds allow small investors to reap the benefits once enjoyed only by Big Money investors. A mutual fund pools the money from a number of investors and puts the money in stocks, bonds, options, or a combination of financial products. Because the amount of money is much greater when it's pooled, the group can invest in dozens or even hundreds of different companies, so you don't put all your eggs in one basket.

They've got you coming and going. As an investor, you have to help pay for the management and maintenance of the mutual fund. It can be tricky to compare fees, since they aren't all the same:

- *Front-end loads* are commissions you must pay when you get into the fund. These fees typically run 4 to 6 percent, but they can reach as high as 8.5 percent —a significant hit just to join the club. If you invest $1,000 in a fund with an 8.5 percent load, you'll pay $85 off the top before you've earned one penny.
- *Back-end loads* are fees you must pay at the time you withdraw your money. These fees can be hidden by some unscrupulous brokers who might tell you a fund is a no-load fund when, in fact, you must pay a back-end load or a "contingent deferred sales charge" or a "redemption fee" to get your hands on your money. In general, back-end loads vary depending on how long you leave your money in the fund; the sooner you sell, the higher the fee.
- *Management fees* are the periodic fees, usually around 1 percent per year, that you must pay for maintaining your particular account on top of the commissions to get in and out of the fund. This expense

may include the infamous 12b-1 charge, which actually reimburses a mutual fund for its advertising and promotion costs.

No-load funds allow you to avoid sales commissions on the purchase of shares by investing directly with the fund. You can avoid some fees with no-load funds, but you'll still face the management fees.

The magic number. It can be very frustrating to play detective and hunt down a mutual fund's hidden fees, forever fearful that you've overlooked some obscure charge. No need to sweat. Instead, just look for the expense ratio in the fund's prospectus. This number includes all the fund expenses; the lower the number, the better. The lowest funds may have expense ratios of 0.5 percent, the highest over 2 percent.

That's Bull

We can't all be Number 1, now can we? It can be quite confusing if you read the advertisements in financial magazines. Don't believe the claims until you read the fine print. For example, some mutual fund ads may scream "#1" in the headline, but the fine print whispers "among funds of the same type with assets between $500 million and $1 billion." This is yet another example of how to lie with statistics.

Take your chances. Even the most conservative mutual funds present some risk. And investors have become confused now that their banks are offering mutual funds. Make no mistake; money in a mutual fund is not guaranteed by the Federal Deposit Insurance Corporation or the bank, even if it is sold through an insured institution. Bank *deposits* are insured; _investments,_ even those made through a bank, are not. While putting your money in a conservative bond fund is hardly living on the financial edge, it's important to understand that it's also not a sure thing.

Key Lingo

Currently there are more than 4,000 mutual funds eager to take your money off your hands. Different funds have different investment objectives or strategies. Here's a rundown of a few of the most common types:

Stock funds

Aggressive-growth: Funds that invest in stocks of smaller companies that may increase in value rapidly; they accept more risk than regular growth funds.

Balanced: Funds that invest in both stocks and bonds.

Equity-income: Funds that invest in the stocks of well-established companies that pay dividends.

Growth-and-income: Funds that invest in companies that may increase in stock price and provide regular dividends.

Growth: Funds that invest in stocks of smaller companies that have the possibility of increasing in value quickly.

International and global: Funds that invest in both foreign and U.S. stocks.

Bond funds

Corporate (short-term): Funds that invest in corporate bonds with maturities of up to three years; they are the safest of the corporate bond funds.

Corporate (intermediate-term): Funds that invest in corporate bonds with average maturities of four to 10 years; they generally pay a higher return than short-term funds.

Corporate (long-term): Funds that invest in corporate bonds with average maturities of more than 10 years; they carry more risk than intermediate-term funds.

Corporate (high-yield): Funds that invest in "junk" bonds with low ratings, meaning they have a high risk of default; they are the riskiest of the corporate funds.

Government: Funds that invest in U.S. government bonds; they pay lower rates of return than corporate bonds, but they are safer.

Municipal: Funds that invest in bonds issued by state and local governments; they are often free from federal income tax, so they usually yield a lower rate of interest than other bonds. Tax-free bonds can provide a high rate of return, depending on your tax bracket. For example, a fund yielding 4 percent would equal a taxable yield of 5.1 percent for someone in the 28 percent tax bracket or 5.4 percent for someone in the 36 percent tax bracket.

Don't Forget to Ask

☐ Is there a front-end load?

☐ Is there a back-end load?

☐ What are the management or service fees?

☐ What has been the annual yield over the last five years after deducting all expenses?

☐ What is the fund's investment philosophy or strategy?

☐ How did this fund's performance compare with others of the same size and investment strategy? Is that information published somewhere?

■ GETTING YOUR MONEY'S WORTH FROM A FINANCIAL PLANNER

A good financial planner can help you develop a workable strategy to meet your financial goals. A bad one can waste a lot of time and money by charging excessive fees and by steering you toward investments that don't meet your needs. So what are you supposed to do?

Who pays the piper? When choosing a planner, look carefully at how that person is paid.

- *Commission-only* planners make their money by collecting a commission on the investments they recommend, such as insurance policies, mutual funds, and securities. Proceed with caution: These planners only make money if you invest, and they may steer you toward investments that pay the highest commissions. They may act in their best interest, not yours.

- *Fee plus commission* planners charge a fee to set up your plan, and they get additional commissions if you make investments through them.

- *Fee-offset* planners will charge a fee to set up the plan, but any commission they earn on investments you make through them will offset the fee.

- *Fee-only* planners tend to cost more up front, but they won't get any kind of kickback or commission on your investments. Expect to pay a pretty penny for the advice: Fees can be several thousand dollars for a plan, whether based on a percentage of your assets or as an hourly wage of $50 to $200.

- *Salaried* planners are paid by the banks, credit unions, and other financial institutions that offer financial advice to their members. While these planners aren't getting any kind of commission on your investments, they probably won't encourage you to withdraw your money from their institution and put it somewhere else, so once again be aware of the bias.

Expert advice. Or is it? There are no statutory professional, educational, or licensing requirements for financial planners. Hey, just ask your know-it-all neighbor and you'll get an earful of financial advice. Fewer than one out of five of the nation's so-called financial planners have gone to the trouble to meet the standards or requirements of a professional organization for financial planners. Those that do may advertise the fact with a series of letters following their name, such as CFP (certification from the Institute of Certified Financial Planners) or ChFC (certification from the American Society of Chartered Financial Consultants). Credentials are no guarantee of competence, but they don't hurt.

Don't Forget to Ask

- ☐ How are you compensated?
- ☐ What is your investment philosophy? Conservative? Aggressive?
- ☐ What investments do you specialize in?
- ☐ What are your professional affiliations?
- ☐ What kind of professional training or education do you have in financial planning?
- ☐ Do you personally research the products you recommend?
- ☐ How often will we meet to prepare my plan?
- ☐ What kind of follow-up will there be?
- ☐ May I have a list of references?

■ TAKING STOCK: SELECTING A BROKER

A lot of people talk about "making a killing" in the stock market, but there are plenty of other, less outspoken, investors who die a slow, lingering death. In general, money invested in the stock market will appreciate in value faster than the rate of inflation, but there are no guarantees.

It's not all a matter of luck. Sure, playing the market is a sophisticated form of gambling, but it's up to you to decide how much to hedge your bets. You can invest in conservative stocks that are apt to do very well over the years with minimal risk, or you can invest aggressively and put your money in riskier stocks that have the potential of paying back large rewards. The choice is yours.

Buying advice. When selecting a broker, you must first decide how much advice you want:

- *Full-service brokers* charge a commission of 3 to 5 percent on each transaction. This money goes, they say, to compensate brokers for their expert investment advice.
- *Discount brokers* charge a commission equal to 50 to 70 percent less than a full-service broker, but they do not offer any advice or recommendations. You call the shots.

Let's make a deal. A full-service broker doesn't have to charge you the full commission, and many are willing to negotiate rather than lose your business. Even though they don't want you to know it, most brokers can charge 20 to 30 percent less than the top rate without getting special approval from upper management. There can be a lot of variation in fees since some brokers offer lower rates on large accounts, and others give a break to clients who enter into smaller transactions. The only way to find out how much you'd have to pay in commissions on your account is to ask.

That's Bull

When opening a brokerage account, you may be asked to sign a waiver that states that any disputes that might arise will be settled by arbitration rather than in court. What the fine print doesn't say is that the arbitration panel consists of representatives of the securities industry. You probably won't want to take a case before a federal district court jury, but you don't want to give up that right either. To protect your rights, simply cross out the offending language before you sign the form. A broker may try to tell you that you have to sign the form, but see if the story changes if you threaten to take your money elsewhere.

Whose side are you on? When dealing with a broker, keep in mind that he or she only makes money when you buy or sell stock. In addition to the commission, some brokers collect additional cash by earning an underwriting fee or incentive for selling certain stocks that are being pushed at that particular time. Some brokerage houses even conduct contests with prizes such as a two-week vacation in Hawaii to the brokers who sell the most of a particular stock. As an investor, you must always ask yourself: What does my broker have to gain if I follow this advice?

Trust your mother. But only trust your stockbroker if she moonlights as your mom. Many brokers offer ''discretionary'' accounts, which authorize the broker to buy or sell stocks on their behalf without specific authorization for each transaction. Don't do it.

I remember it like it was yesterday. The you-said/I-said game is annoying under the best of circumstances, but it becomes downright dangerous when you're talking about your financial investments. Don't depend on your memory or your broker's statements to confirm your buy and sell orders; take notes during all your conversations with your broker and confirm your statements against these written records.

So how are we doing? Most people love their brokers in a bull market, and consider them crooks when the market turns against them. The best way to assess your broker's performance (rather than the performance of the market as a whole) is to check the percentage change in the value of your portfolio against the percentage change in the Standard & Poor's 500 Index, which is a measure of five hundred leading stocks. If your money is consistently performing worse than the market as a whole, then you should consider finding another broker.

I knew you were a crook. Too often it's too late when you figure out what kind of person you've trusted with your money. But you can now find out *before* handing over your money whether a broker has had a history of fraud and consumer complaints. Check with the North American Securities Administrators Association and your state securities commission. You should be able to get a computer printout of your broker's professional profile and history.

Don't Forget to Ask

Before investing with any stockbroker, take time to interview a few and see which one best reflects your financial philosophy and willingness to take risks. If a broker isn't willing to take the time to tell you about his or her services in a relaxed and unrushed manner, then chances are you won't get any more time when the broker has your money. During the interview, be sure to ask the following:

☐ *How long have you been with this brokerage firm?*
☐ *How long have you been in the securities business?*

☐ *Where did you learn about finance?*

☐ *Can you supply a certified history of your investment and research recommendations? Of your firm's recommendations?*

☐ *Where do you get your investment recommendations? Do you work with a research department? Do you do your own research? Do you consult with friends?*

☐ *How many industries and companies does your firm follow?*

☐ *What kind of statements will I receive on my investments? How often?*

☐ *How high are the commissions? Are these rates flexible?*

☐ *In addition to commissions, are there any additional charges for securities safekeeping or account management?*

☐ *What is your overall investment philosophy? What kind of firms do you invest in?*

☐ *What is your general philosophy about sell advice and profit taking?*

☐ *How many clients do you service? How many does your firm service?*

☐ *Do you have any client references?*

☐ *How quickly do you return phone calls?*

☐ *Have you ever been subject to any professional disciplinary actions or criminal convictions?*

Don't just accept the broker's word on the last question. Make a call to the National Association of Securities Dealers in Washington, D.C. You can get a report listing disciplinary actions, criminal convictions, and arbitration decisions that have been made against the broker or the firm. (It won't list pending cases or consumer complaints, however.) In addition, you can check with the state securities commission for any additional information.

Chapter Four

PAINTING THE
TOWN RED

■ HOT TICKETS: BUYING TICKETS TO THE THEATER

Whether on Broadway or Main Street, if you want to see the show—and you don't want to do it as an usher—you're going to need a ticket. The fine art of procuring theater tickets varies from city to city, but these tips generally apply:

Try calling the box office. It's a dandy place to start, and a great way to avoid the service fees slapped on by ticket services. Better yet, stop by the theater and pick up the tickets yourself. This is your golden opportunity to check out the seating arrangement so that you know what you're buying.

Sit with the V.I.P.s. Every theater has "house tickets," which are given to producers, friends of cast members, reviewers from the press, and other V.I.P.s. House tickets that aren't given to the elite are sold to the public—sometimes at reasonable prices. Call the box office and ask when they release the house seats. If they say 10:00 A.M. on the day of the show, sit by your phone and start dialing at 9:59 A.M.

So, do these tickets go on sale? Well, don't ask about a sale but do ask about discounts. Some theaters cut prices for students and senior citizens. On the day of the show, some theaters slice the price on all their tickets for all comers. It can't hurt to ask.

Is there an outlet mall for the theater district?
Some large metropolitan areas have special half-price ticket
outlets. Ask the theater or check with the visitor's information service for the city to see if the service is provided in
that area.

Go ahead, move up in the world. Though you
might annoy those people sitting next to you who actually
paid $85 for their tickets, there's nothing wrong with
switching to a better seat after intermission—as long as
you're sure nobody else is sitting there. Still, you need to
be prepared to go back to your assigned seat if an usher
catches you and wags a finger in your direction. If you get
caught, hang your head in shame—then try it again next
time.

**If only you could set up a folding chair in the
back.** Of course, standing room means just that—no folding chairs allowed. But standing room can mean huge savings, as well as a ticket to an otherwise sold-out show. Most
often *somebody* doesn't show, so you can fill those empty
seats after intermission. The catch: You can't get standing-
room tickets until all the sitting-room tickets have been sold.

Make a scene. If you're unhappy with your seat, ask
to speak to the box-office manager. Perhaps the clerk in the
box office forgot to tell you that the seats were "obstructed
view" or maybe the cleaning people left upholstery fluid on
your seat and it caused you to break out in itchy hives during
the first act (this actually happened). You're not being a
prima donna; consider it comparable to sending back the
wine or steak in a restaurant. Most professional theaters will
either refund the sum of the ticket or give you free tickets.
If you've got a legitimate gripe, you might just find that it
pays to complain.

The show must go on. When it's showtime, the
curtain goes up. If you're willing to stay flexible about your
evening plans, you can check with the box office just before

the show starts on the chance that there will be some tickets left. Of course, you'll have to settle for the leftovers, which could either be orchestra seats or the last row of the second balcony.

■ How to Get the Best Table in a Restaurant

When you go out to eat, you may want to sit at the table next to the window overlooking the bay. Or you may prefer the privacy and quiet of dining in the secluded back room. Or you may opt for a spot where you can both see and be seen. Getting a good table in a restaurant means different things to different people, so you'll have to let the maître d' know what you have in mind. The best way to ensure getting a table at the time you want is to make a reservation. You can ask for a specific room or area, but most restaurants won't make promises.

Think of a restaurant as an airline. When you're rushing to catch a plane, you know that the pilot won't wait, even if there was an accident on the highway, the parking lot was full, and the escalator didn't work. The airline won't wait, and neither will the maître d'. If you're late for a reservation, save the excuses. Don't expect to show up at 7:15 for a 6:15 reservation and expect to find your table waiting for you. Most reservations are held only fifteen minutes beyond the allotted hour.

Even Prince Charming gets help from the maître d'. If you're planning some enchanted evening, let the restaurant staff know. It's the restaurateur's job to anticipate your desires, but even the world's finest maître d' isn't clairvoyant. So if it's your wife's fortieth birthday or you're planning to propose marriage or you will be conducting an important business meeting between bites, keep the maître d' informed. You'll probably get a table more suited to the atmosphere you're searching for, and who knows, you may get some special service, too.

It's OK as long as the maître d' isn't an undercover cop or a moonlighting federal judge. If you want to bribe the maître d' to move your name to the top of the waiting list or to ensure that you get a room with a view, then go ahead and slip him or her a few bucks. Do it just like the smooth-talkers on TV: Put the cash in the palm of your hand, shake hands with the maître d', and pass the bill while saying, "I know it's very busy, but anything you can do would be appreciated." Hint: Be discreet. If you make a big show of it, everyone will know what you're doing and the maître d' won't be able to help you. Another hint: Use $10 and $20 bills. If you hand over a single, you're apt to wind up in the smoking section next to the noisiest waiters' station.

Break it up, break it up. If your relatives are in from out of town and you want a table for ten, you can't be choosy. Most restaurants don't put their large crowds in the choice sections. However, if you're willing to divide into two or three neighboring tables, you may get "better" tables and faster service.

You can't always eat when you're hungry. When it comes to large groups (six or more) many restaurants have two seatings a night. You may not get to eat at 7:30 or 8:00, because that kills the night. Remember, the restaurant is in business to sell food to as many people as possible during the evening.

Rely on someone else's reputation. If you're staying in a hotel with a concierge on staff, allow him or her to do the tedious task of making reservations for you. (You're on vacation, remember.) Not only will you have one less thing to worry about, but you're apt to get a better table than you would if you called on your own; the restaurant will want to keep the hotel's guests happy so that the recommendations will continue.

■ CHEERS: BUYING BUBBLY

When the cork pops and the bubbles start to dance in the glass, you know it's time to celebrate. Champagne is the festive, feel-good wine that says "Happy New Year," "a toast for the bride and groom," or "congratulations" in a way no ordinary wine can manage.

Champagne is the unique mixture of white wines that acquires its characteristic bubbles when it ferments a second time in a stoppered bottle. A number of countries bottle bubbly, but there is only one true champagne: the stuff bottled and shipped from France's Champagne region, where the soil conditions and climate combine to provide the ideal setting for growing the pinot noir, pinot meunier, and Chardonnay grapes used in champagne.

Alas, there will never be enough real champagne to quench the world's thirst. This 75,000-acre growing area simply can't produce enough grapes to meet the 2-billion-bottle worldwide demand for sparkling wine, so similar sparkling wines are produced in other areas, including the United States. American winemakers can label their sparkling wine "champagne" as long as the label discloses the location of origin, making it possible to have Napa Valley Champagne, which, when you think about it, defies logic, not to mention geography.

Before diving in, you should become familiar with a few basic types of champagne:

- *Blanc de blancs* are white wines made only from white Chardonnay grapes; they tend to be lighter. The typical champagne is a blend of about two-thirds red grapes and one-third white grapes.
- *Cuvees de prestige* are the flagship bottles that represent the best the champagne house can offer; the best of the best.
- *Nonvintage* champagnes are blends of the current year and reserved wines that produce balanced tastes unique to the house; about 85 percent total champagne production is nonvintage.
- *Rose or pink champagne* is blended with a small amount of red wine for "blush."
- *Tete de cuvee* is champagne made from the first pressing of the grapes. This is a superior blend—often placed in a specially designed bottle—that often costs twice as much as nonvintage wine from the same house.
- *Vintage* is a premium-priced champagne made of grapes from a single year's harvest when the grapes are exceptional, usually due to an unusual amount of sunshine.

You can spend less than $20 for a bottle of champagne on sale, or more than $200 for a rare bottle of 1983 Krug "Clos du Mesnil." For under $50 a bottle, Veuve Clicquot and Roederer provide a lively champagne with a lot of character, as does the less well-known brand Henri Abele, the champagne served at the French embassy. Whatever your price range, you can appear to be a serious oenophile by imbibing only the best.

Hey, this must be the good stuff. At its best, champagne is fermented in the bottle, though some cheap brands ferment the wine in bulk and then transfer it to individual bottles or actually add carbonation directly. Check the bottle for the words "Methode champenoise" or the statement "fermented in this bottle" to indicate the proper process for preparing champagne.

Just like in the movies. If you're serious about champagne, you need a champagne bucket filled with ice and a bit of water to chill the bottle for thirty to forty-five minutes (warm bottles foam more, as do those that have been shaken). Pulling the bottle out of the fridge is not only less romantic, but if the neck of the bottle gets too cold, the cork won't announce itself with that glorious "pop" and the dramatic show of fizz.

Trivia to Impress Your Friends

Actions speak louder than words. And when it comes to opening champagne, style is everything. To look like a pro, you should tip the well-chilled bottle to a 45-degree angle, then remove the wire cage and loosen the cork, keeping a thumb over it to prevent it from shooting out. Gently turn the bottle, not the cork. If the cork goes ballistic, you blew it. Likewise, if you allow a foamy head to spew all over the floor, you not only look like a dolt, but you've wasted precious champagne. Perhaps you should practice a few times in the privacy of your home before trying to impress your friends and loved ones.

Never use a "champagne" glass for champagne. Sounds odd, but the quintessential wide-mouth champagne glass lets the bubbles dissipate too quickly. Victorian restaurateurs and caterers introduced these shallow glasses because they were easier to fill than narrow-rimmed versions (and they also figured they could make those nifty champagne fountains by piling them up). Instead, use either a glass slipper, or the next best thing: flutes or long, thin, egg- or tulip-shaped stemware, which will showcase the bubbles.

Expect a chilly reception. And lousy bubbles if you chill the glasses before serving champagne. The glasses will become damp and this will dampen the effervescence. Also be sure the glasses are spotless; a hint of dishwashing detergent, sheeting agent, or degreaser can affect the bubbles. Of course, you should drink from only the finest crystal: Champagne should be a feast for the eyes as well as the lips.

Good to the last drop. The typical bottle of champagne will provide six to eight servings. If you can't quite make it to the bottom, recork the bottle using a champagne stopper and slip it in the fridge. Try to finish it within one week; it will lose its fizz every time you open it, so let the party continue.

Bottoms up. Most champagne producers release their wines when they consider them ready to drink. Nonvintage champagnes won't improve with age; instead, after four or five years they will take on a hazelnut and coffee taste as they slowly grow darker and lose their fizz. While waiting, keep bottles on their sides in a cool, dark place. Surely you have something to celebrate, so get the champagne flutes and think up a toast.

Key Lingo

Champagnes range in taste from very dry to sweet. Keep in mind, however, that a true champagne aficionado would frown on anything sweeter than Brut.

Ultra-brut: *No additional sugar has been added after fermentation.*

Brut: *Contains no more than 1 percent sugar.*

Extra sec *or* **extra dry:** *Contains 1 to 2 percent sugar.*

Sec *or* **dry:** *Contains 3 to 6 percent sugar.*

Demi sec: *Contains 5 to 10 percent sugar.*

■ It's More Than Grape Juice: Choosing Cheap (But Good) Wine

Stripped of romance and sophistication, wine is nothing more than fermented grape juice in which sugar has been transformed into alcohol. Ah, but when you sip a glass of smooth, full-bodied red or white wine, you know that something magical happens between the grape on the vine and the glass before you.

When buying wine, price isn't necessarily an indicator of quality. You can spend as little as $3.50 or several hundred dollars for a bottle of wine. Of course, truly superb wines are expensive, but not all expensive wines are necessarily superb.

Can you turn this wine back into water? Actually, these days it's not so easy to find bad wine. Sure, some wines are better than others, but winemakers now have a considerably better understanding and more control over the fermentation process than they did in the past. Still, it's virtually impossible to turn bad grapes into good wine. If you're not sure about what to buy, ask the clerk at a reputable shop and then try a couple of bottles. Odds are you won't find vinegar in any bottle you sample.

It was a very good year . . . But this is a very bad wine. Vintage cards are like crib sheets for wine buffs. They are pocket-sized cards that list the growing conditions in different parts of the world and the wine quality on a year-by-year basis. For example, a card might indicate that the 1982 vintage in Bordeaux was superb and the 1984 vintage was poor. But that's still no guarantee of quality. Don't rely on a vintage card alone; good wines have been bottled in bad years—and bad wines in good years.

I know what I like. And it's not always what the experts like. The major wine magazines, including *Wine*

Spectator, *Wine Advocate,* and *Wine & Spirits,* all use rating systems to assess the quality of certain wines. Go ahead and read the magazines as a guide, but keep in mind that these ratings reflect the taste and preferences of the trained panel of experts. The experts may say a particular bottle of wine is good, but your palate may not agree. Buy what you like; you're the one who's going to drink it.

Key Lingo

When it comes to making wine, all grapes are not created equal. Any of the nearly 8,000 different types of grape theoretically can be fermented and turned to wine, but only about 50 varieties produce top-quality wines. These are a few of the most common:

Cabernet sauvignon: *A full-bodied wine with noticeable tannins or astringency; it ages well.*

Chardonnay: *A dry wine used in Chablis and champagne; it can have a wide range of flavors, depending on how it's blended.*

Chenin blanc: *A light, well-balanced wine that tends to be relatively sweet.*

Merlot: *A medium-bodied red wine, somewhat softer and lighter than cabernet sauvignon, that does not require as much aging to develop its full taste.*

Pinot noir: *This "noblest vine of all" produces a light- to medium-bodied red wine that is complex and rich. It is often used in the best champagnes.*

Sauvignon blanc: *A popular white wine often served with fish and shellfish; it is known for its herbal flavors.*

Zinfandel: *A vine of unknown origin that produces a berrylike, zesty flavor; often mixed with white wines to form the rose or blush wine known as white zinfandel.*

Before you take the plunge . . . Before buying a bottle or case of wine, go to a restaurant with a good wine list and staff. Explore a number of wines by the glass, then buy by the bottle.

Make a party of it. If you want to sample a wide range of wines and learn more about the subtleties of wine tasting, go to a wine festival or fair. You might also consider joining a local wine club—some are pretentious, others aren't. (You can always go and fake it.)

Sweet talker. Actually, most people talk dry but drink sweet. Keep this in mind when buying wine for guests. Fruity is a term used to refer to wines that are a bit less sweet.

Running hot and cold. The "proper" temperature to serve a wine depends on the type. White and blush wines are usually chilled to about 45 degrees (the temperature inside most refrigerators or attained by submerging a bottle in ice water for thirty minutes). Remember, the colder the wine, the less you will be able to appreciate its taste and smell. Most reds are served at room temperature; red wines that are too cold often seem tart or astringent.

Tomorrow and tomorrow and tomorrow. Even in the refrigerator, an open bottle of wine doesn't keep long. Wine shops and gourmet stores sell special wine caps that extend the life of a bottle of open wine. There are two basic types: the vacuum type that sucks out the air before stopping the bottle (cost: $7 to $10 or so), and the carbon dioxide blanket type that injects a thin layer of carbon dioxide gas into the bottle (cost: $20 to $60, plus replacement gas cartridges). Without a special stopper, wine—red or white—will last only a day or two in the refrigerator. With the fancy stoppers, it will last three or four days.

Aged to perfection. Unfortunately, older isn't necessarily better—at least when it comes to wine. Some wines, especially red wines, need time to mature, but others can spoil after as little as a year or two. There are no generalities; ask the shopkeeper about storage if you're in doubt.

Cheaper by the dozen. You can save money— usually about 10 percent—by buying wine by the case. But before you stock your wine cellar (or closet, as the case may be) buy a single bottle and see how much you really like it. Don't blindly follow the liquor store owner's lead, especially if there's a special discount on the stuff you're considering.

Just ask the butler to pick up a bottle from the wine cellar. What, no butler? No wine cellar? Then, like the rest of us, you'll have to substitute some other quiet spot to store your wine. You're looking for a spot that remains a constant temperature and experiences minimal vibration and exposure to light. Ideally, your grotto for storing wine should remain at 55 to 58 degrees with a relative humidity of 65 to 70 percent. An unused fireplace fitted with racks for bottles can work well.

Lie down and relax. Not you, the wine. Wine bottles that will be kept for more than a couple of weeks should be stored on their sides so that the corks don't dry out, shrink, and allow air to leak into the bottle.

And my filet mignon is overcooked, too. So what is that bottle-opening ritual at fine restaurants really about? It's a way for you to check to see if there is anything wrong with the bottle of wine that's being served, as well as to make sure you're pleased with the wine you have selected in more general terms. The wine steward or sommelier (French for wine waiter) will open the bottle at the table and pour about half an inch of wine into your glass. You're first checking to see if the bottle is ''corky'' or spoiled. You don't need any special skills to do this; if the bottle is bad you'll get a waft of musty aroma long before you take a sip. Only a dork would smell the cork, but you might want to look it over because it will be stamped with the vineyard name and location. Next you swish the sample around in the glass for a moment, then you taste. If you don't care for your selection, fake it rather than make a scene. Most restaurants won't allow you to return a sound wine simply because you don't like it. (If you want revenge, you can refuse to order dessert.)

■ DON'T GET STUCK ON FORMALITIES: RENTING A TUXEDO

A survey done by the International Formalwear Association found that a majority of men think women pay more attention to men in tuxes than in suits. Whether this is true or not, tuxedos are certainly a chance for the well-dressed man to reveal his sartorial savvy. Then again, it could be his downfall. Why accept a look that says "dressed up but rented" when "elegant, sophisticated and sexy" doesn't have to cost a penny more?

Look for early signs of aging. When renting a tuxedo, price isn't everything. Low-cost tuxes sometimes look as if they have spent too many evenings slow dancing at the high school prom. Early signs of too many long nights: The satin on the lapels won't lay flat and the fabric-covered buttons have started to fray at the edges.

Polyester is (still) out. Bargain formalwear often comes in a wide variety of polyester and synthetic fibers. If you want to look like Fred Astaire, stick to suits made of 100 percent wool; they will hang better, feel better, and look better on you. When calling around to compare prices, ask the shopkeeper whether the suits are made of polyester or wool.

Grooming the groomsmen. At group events, such as weddings, be sure to rent all the tuxedos from the same location. Slight variations in lapel design, ties, or ascots often separate formalwear from one store and another. Inquire about group discounts. Many stores offer a rent-six-get-one-free deal (or some variation), but only if you ask.

At most formalwear rental outfits, it only takes ten to fifteen minutes for someone to take your measurements and fill out the paperwork. Be sure to allow plenty of time for last-minute alterations when you pick up the suit. You don't have to feel like a stuffed penguin to look good; you should feel comfortable, if a bit formal.

"To Complete the Look . . . " (Which is more of an option than you might think.)

- There are so many *shirts* to choose from, so few ways to go wrong. Except, of course, your own business shirt. And do forget about the ruffled styles. If someone trots it out, send it back. John Travolta hasn't ruled the dance floor in a while.

- Purists demand *shoes* in patent leather. Details! Details! You can wear your own more comfortable (freshly polished) dress shoes. The key here is to wear dress shoes with as *little* design on the toe cap as possible. But don't wear brown shoes with a black tux. You'll look as if either you or the store ran out.

- *Cummerbunds and ties* can run the gamut from black to solid colors to prints to sequins or handpainted works of art. You don't *need* anything but basic black. Still, you may want to express yourself. It's up to you (and your date) to decide what's funky and what's over-the-line.

- *Suspenders* (a.k.a. "braces" for formalwear insiders) are hidden from view until it's time to let down your guard and slip out of your jacket. Which you may not do, so why bother. Then again, they do come in everything from latex rubber to three-dimensional vegetables. You might think of all sorts of other uses for them. (Tip: Unless you're headed for a grocer's convention, forgo the vegetable suspenders.)

Classic Bull

Capes, canes, and **top hats** are often suggested. Of course the salesperson may forget to ask if you're attending a Halloween party dressed as a vampire or Abe Lincoln. So do set him straight. Not that he'll back off, but you should.

■ QUEEN FOR A NIGHT: RENTING AN EVENING GOWN

With the assistance of a Fairy Godmother and the wave of a magic wand, Cinderella's tattered rags were transformed into a stunning ball gown. Unless you have your own Fairy Godmother, you'll probably have to settle for assistance from a formalwear specialty shop and the wave of a MasterCard or VISA. Putting on the ritz means putting out some cash, whether you rent or buy your formal garb.

What price beauty? Renting formal regalia isn't cheap. Most bridal and formalwear shops will try to make back what they pay for a dress in one or two wearings. A dress that you'd pay $800 for retail probably would cost the shop owner $400 or $500 wholesale. To rent it, you will pay $200 to $350, even though after your night on the town you'll be left with nothing but memories and a credit card bill. Before renting, check out the clearance rack at a formalwear store, just in case you see something that strikes your fancy. It may not cost any more to buy than to rent.

Evening gowns aren't exactly wash-and-wear. The reason renting gowns is so pricey is that it doesn't take long for all those sequins and pearls to look dull and drab. Most dresses start looking a bit tired after just a couple of wearings. Don't just shop for style; look closely for broken beads, sequins without sparkle, and pearls that have lost their luster. Check the seams for frayed threads and signs of obvious alterations.

Don't expect to look like the mannequin. That skintight number may not fit you like a glove, even if your body actually deserves it. Unless you can wear clothes right off the rack, your dress probably won't provide a custom fit. Most women's formalwear is made of delicate fabrics that don't weather alterations very well. The shopkeeper may not be willing to take a tuck here or let out a seam there, since someone else will be wearing the same dress next weekend and she may need everything changed back. Remember, we're not talking about rental tuxes, which are designed to be altered and realtered every weekend. Women's gowns are made of the same silks, satins, and taffetas as gowns for purchase. In addition, a lot of decorative trims and fabric patterns limit the ability to make changes.

Don't feel depressed when you read the label. Most formalwear tends to run small. If you normally wear a size 10, don't cringe when you discover that you need to rent a size 12 or 14 in order to zip up the back. Forget the label and look in the mirror; if you look dumpy, blame it on the dress and choose a more flattering style.

Most shops will rent anything but a date. If

you've rummaged through your jewelry box and just can't find your 2-carat diamond pendant or triple-strand cultured pearl choker, you're in luck. Many shops also rent faux jewelry, in addition to shawls, hairpieces, shoes, and "foundation garments" such as slips and bras. If you're a bit squeamish about sharing your underwear with strangers, shell out $20 or $30 for your own strapless bra. You'll feel better in the morning.

Doesn't your sister have a dress like that? Go ahead, borrow a dress from a friend or relative. Most people won't recognize the threads, especially since they'll look so much better on you.

Don't Forget to Ask

☐ *How many times will this dress be rented between now and the date of my event?*

☐ *When can I come in to inspect the dress after the last rental?*

☐ *Can I get my money back if I'm not happy with the appearance of the dress when I pick it up?*

☐ *When can I pick up the dress?*

☐ *When do I have to return it?*

☐ *Is there an extra charge for returning it late?*

☐ *Is this dress for sale?*

Chapter Five

"I COULD USE A VACATION"

■ ALMOST HOME: FINDING A SUITABLE HOTEL ROOM

Hotels and motels try to be accommodating, but they don't always succeed. Sure, in slow times they offer special rates and bend over backward to lure you to their vacant rooms, but other times they overbook rooms and leave guests without a roof over their heads. When you're tired of traveling and looking for a room—with or without a view—you aren't in the mood to hear any excuses.

Prepare to play the numbers game. You might have reserved the room six months ago, but so what? It's the confirmation number that can be critical when it comes to getting the hotel to honor your reservation. (Some states actually require a hotel to give you a room if you have a confirmation number.) Insist that your travel agent give you the actual hotel confirmation number. Beware: A travel agent's voucher is the weakest form of proof. It lacks official acknowledgment from the hotel.

Is the couch in the lobby a sleep sofa? You don't want to have to snooze in the hotel foyer, but you might have to threaten to set up camp if the hotel is unwilling to honor your confirmed reservation. Don't hesitate to express —in loud tones, if necessary—your displeasure at losing your room. Rooms have a way of materializing for those who demand them loudly. If there is no room at the inn, most reputable hotels will try to find alternate accommodations, though you have no guarantee of comparable price or quality.

Trivia to Impress Your Friends

Gideon Bibles were first placed in hotels in 1908 in the Superior Hotel in Superior, Montana, after local pastors asked that Bibles be available to travelers. They are now in hotel rooms in nearly 150 countries worldwide.

You won't have to make your bed in the morning. And neither will the hotel maid if you never make it to your room. If you've guaranteed payment for your room you will have to pay for it even if you never show up. That's the price you pay for a guaranteed room—it's yours no matter what hour you appear. You can cancel a guaranteed reservation if your plans change, but you might have to call a day or two in advance.

For you, we have a special deal. Flip through your wallet and you should be able to find a credit card, membership card, business card, or other credential that makes you eligible for a discount. Ask about corporate rates, senior citizen or student discounts, or any other special deals. If you travel frequently, consider signing up for a frequent-stay program, some of which are in cahoots with airline frequent-flier offers. If you have no scruples, you might look on a noticeboard at the hotel and look for conventions. Pick the biggest and say you're with the convention.

Timing is everything. Business travelers go home on weekends, emptying busy hotels. Check into weekend discounts, which are often available at hotels and resorts that cater to business travelers during the week. Some packages include discounts of 30 percent, and may also include bonuses such as theater tickets, drinks, and tours.

Forget the middleman. Skip the call to the company's national reservation line and call the hotel directly. You'll probably get a better rate, and there will be more room for negotiation. Some hotels change their rates almost daily, depending on current occupancy. Remember, hotel rooms are perishable goods; if the room sits empty for the night, that lost income can't be made up. Don't be shy. Ask the reservationist, "Is this the best rate I can get?"

Thanks for the fresh towels and for making the bed. That's basically what you're saying when you tip the housekeeper. It's common to leave $1 a day on the dresser every day; don't assume you can save your singles and just leave $7 at the end of the week, because you will probably have a different room keeper each night.

You might not want to keep your valuables under the mattress. Instead, for safekeeping, drop off items with the receptionist in the lobby to store in the hotel safe. Don't trust the room safes, which may be found in the closets of luxury hotels. Many states require hotels to insure goods stored in the hotel safe but not those items stashed in room safes.

Pack a bag of pretzels before you leave home. Or make a trip to a local convenience store. Or go hungry. Do whatever you can to avoid hotel "mini-bars," which charge exorbitant rates for snacks, soft drinks, and alcoholic beverages. If you must indulge, wake up early and run to the store and replace what you've consumed during the late-night munchies, as long as you can find the exact brand and size package.

You might as well walk outside to a pay phone. Some hotels impose outrageous surcharges to use the phone, even for local and toll-free calls. For example, some alternative operator services charge higher rates than the more common carriers, such as AT&T, MCI, and Sprint. In some cases, the hotels choose these carriers because they split the profits generated by the excessive charges. The hotels must post the phone rates, so find out how much the call will cost before you decide to phone home.

Key Lingo

Some wayward travelers use the terms "hotel" and "motel" interchangeably, but they aren't the same. A hotel has a lobby and enclosed hallways; a motel allows travelers to walk directly from their cars to the door of their rooms.

■ HOLDING THE BAG: BUYING LUGGAGE

One of the biggest hassles of travel is dealing with your luggage. First, you must contend with the organizing and the packing, then you must endure the backbreaking chore of lugging your stuff from one place to another. They don't call it lug-gage for nothing.

When shopping for luggage, expect to spend at least $100 for a full-sized suitcase, though you can easily spend more than $600 for an aluminum Zero Halliburton hard-side case. As for garment bags, you can spend less than $50 for a bare-bones vinyl garment bag, or more than $200 for a bag with more pockets, nicer hardware, and leather instead of vinyl trim.

On the sides. Soft-side or hard-side? It's a matter of

personal preference. Hard-sided suitcases are made of either polypropylene or metal, or they are box-constructed, meaning they are a metal or wood frame covered with leather, vinyl, or fabric. They usually have a combination or key lock. Soft-sided cases are lighter and somewhat expandable, but they provide less crush-resistance.

Carrying on. If there's any way you can manage to get all your clothes into a single carry-on bag, by all means do it. You can eliminate the possibility of having your suitcase fly to Cleveland when you're on your way to Cancun.

Left holding the bag. Comfort counts, especially when you're lugging around a thirty-five-pound bag. Look for padded handles and straps. The typical hard-side case weighs ten to fifteen pounds, a soft-side case three to five pounds less.

On a roll. One advantage to hard-side bags is that they sometimes come with wheels. Generally, wider wheels roll more smoothly than narrower ones and provide better stability. (No surprises there.)

The cow had a few nicks and scratches. And so will your leather luggage. Seasoned travelers consider a seasoned (read: scuffed) leather bag an object of beauty. Scratches happen. They will enhance the appearance of a quality leather bag, and diminish the appearance of a cheap vinyl one.

To whom it may concern. If your luggage is lost or mistakenly picked up by a stranger at the baggage claim carousel, sooner or later someone is going to open it up and look inside. It can't hurt to enclose a note inside each piece of luggage outlining where you are going and the dates you will be there. This will make it easier for the person reading the note to return your bag.

You don't know what you've got till it's gone. But you better know the contents of your bag if you need to file a claim. Before sending your luggage off on that airline conveyor belt to destinations unknown, be sure you've made an inventory listing the contents of each bag. Of course, you want to keep this list with you, not inside your luggage.

Bring your work with you. Or at least your office address and phone number. Rather than advertise to anyone at the airport that you're going to be out of town, list your office address and phone number on the luggage identification tags. If a bag is lost or stolen, you can always have someone at the office forward the calls to you.

Don't throw away the key. Many people don't bother to lock their luggage. Granted, the flimsy little locks on most bags won't deter a determined thief (in fact, many luggage keys are interchangeable), but the lock can help keep a bag from opening accidentally.

Don't Forget to Ask

Before settling on a piece of luggage, ask yourself the following questions:

☐ *Is the covering fabric made of a tight weave that will prevent snagging? Is it treated for water- and stain-resistance?*

☐ *Is the case reinforced at the corners?*

☐ *Do the sides stay aligned when opened? Do they wiggle when moved?*

☐ *Is the stitching even? Are the stress points double stitched?*

☐ *Do the zippers go around the corners easily?*

☐ *Are the handles comfortable? Are they securely mounted?*

☐ *Are the shoulder straps adjustable? Detachable?*

☐ *Are the pull-straps long enough to allow you to stand tall while pulling them?*

■ OVERCOMING THE FEAR OF BUYING AIRLINE TICKETS

Even travelers who don't have a fear of flying often have a fear of buying airline tickets. There are so many issues to worry about: Is this the best rate I can get? What if I need to change my plans? Will I get credit for my frequent-flier miles?

Don't ask, don't tell. The airline ticket agent isn't going to announce that you paid more for your ticket than the person sitting next to you. If the ticket price drops after you buy your ticket, you may be entitled to reimbursement —but only if you ask. Call or visit a ticket agent a day or two before your flight and ask about the current price of your ticket. To get the lower fare, you'll have to meet some restrictions, such as an advance purchase or a requirement that you stay over a Saturday night at your destination.

Key Lingo

Some people assume that a direct *flight will take them from one airport directly to another. Don't be foolish. There's nothing direct about a direct flight. It can stop 15 times in two hours, but as long as you don't change planes, you're on a direct flight. A* nonstop *flight departs from the airport in your home town and lands at your destination.*

Please, please, please, please, please. You may have to beg and grovel, but you may be able to get your money back if you cancel a nonrefundable ticket shortly after you buy it. Travel agents usually pay for their tickets only once a week. If you buy a nonrefundable ticket and change your plans before the agency pays for the ticket, then the agent could void the ticket without subjecting you to a penalty. The travel agent won't be eager to cooperate—no sale, no 8 percent commission—but it certainly can't hurt to ask for a break.

Don't forget to dress in black. Many airlines offer discount bereavement fares for people who need to travel unexpectedly due to family illness or death. Sometimes verification of the emergency is required; ask a travel agent or airline representative when you make reservations.

That's Bull

In an attempt to lure nervous travelers, some life insurance companies sell special limited-term policies to cover airline travelers. Put away your wallet. For one thing, you should already have enough regular life insurance to meet your needs, and this policy should cover you no matter when or how you die. If you're a bit paranoid and still want some added protection, then buy your plane ticket with a major credit card; many credit card companies provide free life insurance to cardholders who die on flights when the tickets are purchased with the card.

Timing is everything. Airfare can vary significantly depending on the day of the week and the time of day you travel. Generally, fares are lowest on Tuesdays and Wednesdays, and highest on Mondays and Fridays. It may also be cheaper to travel either in the middle of the day or late at night, rather than during business commuting hours.

Two halves don't always equal a whole. Discount super-saver tickets often have restrictions, such as staying over a Saturday night. If your plans don't include a weekend stay, check into the cost of buying two round-trip tickets at the discount rate and using only half of each ticket —one from your home to your destination and the other from your destination to your home. In some cases, the cost of two discount tickets may be less than the cost of a single full-fare ticket.

Last is first and first is last. Most people choose their flights based on the time of departure, assuming that the plane that leaves first will arrive first. Silly, silly, silly. The total flight time depends on the type of aircraft and the number of stops or layovers or connections. Be sure to compare the arrival time as well as the departure time when selecting a flight.

Best seat in the house. Well, on the plane anyway. If you aren't ticketed for first class, then "best" depends on what qualities you find more important. For smoothness, look for a seat over the wings. For quiet, sit up front. For a bit of extra leg room, try for a seat in the aisle with the emergency exit.

To your credit. Pay for your airline tickets with a credit card instead of cash. If the ticket is stolen, it can't be redeemed for a cash refund; instead, the ticket price would be credited directly to your credit card account, so the thief couldn't get his hands on your money.

Protect your images. One trip through an airport X-ray machine won't damage the images on your film, but three or four passes can cause fogging, and additional X-rays can result in overexposure. The X-ray machines for international flights may be even stronger, in which case you should request a hand inspection or invest in a lead pouch to protect your film.

Keep it in the family. If you're given the choice between two similar connecting flights, keep the flights with the same airline. Your connecting flights are more likely to be closer together, and the second flight is more apt to be held if your incoming flight arrives a bit late. In addition, by staying with the same airline, your luggage stands a better chance of making it onto the correct plane.

More Bull

Airport duty-free shops don't always come through with the bargain prices they advertise. Yes, you can avoid state and local taxes as well as import duties, but the retailer has to cover the high rent somehow. Before you buy, know how much you would pay at a discount retailer outside the airport.

■ ALL ABOARD: CHOOSING A CRUISE

A cruise ship is like a floating hotel, only at this hotel all your meals, snacks, and on-board entertainment are "free." (Actually you pay dearly for them, only the price is folded into the all-encompassing ticket price.) Without the need to carry a wallet and pay for incidentals, you can lay back and relax; your ship has come in.

It can't hurt to ask. Travel agents enjoy a standard commission of about 10 percent on cruise tickets. On top of that, agents who do a high volume of sales earn the title "preferred supplier" and collect additional bonuses, too. This can work for or against you: The agent may try to steer you to a cruise that you don't really want. Or, on the other hand, you may be able to get a rebate or break on the price by convincing the agent to share some part of the commission with you, especially if the agent is eager to get the booking. When negotiating price, ask about free airfare to the port of departure and free tickets for a third or fourth passenger. Since different agents will have different relationships with the cruise lines, compare the deals you can get at several travel agencies.

Do you have plans for this weekend? How about a seven-day cruise? Discount agencies can offer deep discounts on last-minute bookings. If you can afford to be flexible, you can save 50 to 60 percent off the regular ticket price.

Take the money and run. Before signing a contract, carefully read all the fine print. Where will your money be kept between the time you pay for your tickets and the time you board the cruise ship? Some states require cruise operators to set up an escrow account or to post bond so that ticketholders will be sure to get their money back if the trip is canceled for any reason. Make sure you have this protection before you sign.

It's not just sea sickness. It's sickness at sea. Any cruise ship with more than fifty passengers must have a licensed physician on board, but there's no guarantee that this M.D. would be your doctor of choice if you weren't stranded in the middle of the Atlantic. If you have any special medical needs, check with the travel agent about the training and experience of the ship's doctor before you cast off.

Are you a member of the Reindeer Lodge? If not, then you may not want to travel with a herd of Reindeer Lodge members. Cruise ships often book large groups. No problem, unless the group is large enough to dominate a dining room or other facilities. Ask your travel agent whether any clubs or groups have signed up for the cruise you're considering. If the agent isn't sure, call the cruise line directly.

You missed the boat. Now what are you supposed to do? You can spare yourself the anxiety of close connections by booking a cruise that includes airfare. If a connecting flight is delayed or canceled and you aren't at the dock when it's time to shove off, then the cruise line must get you to the ship, even if you have to fly to the ship's first port of call.

A room with a view. To minimize the chances of coming down with motion sickness, choose a cabin near the waterline in the center of the ship. These rooms will probably cost less than deck staterooms, anyway.

You're going to dance until dawn. But not until the orchestra or band starts up. If you plan to partake of the evening's entertainment, then book the second seating for dinner. You'll have more time to get ready and less time to wait before the late-night activities begin.

Lost at sea. When booking your first cruise, make it a short one. Cruising isn't for everyone, and you don't want to be surrounded by saltwater when you discover that you'd rather be reclining in an easy chair at home.

Chapter Six

THE ELEGANT
PURCHASE
(AFFORDING THE
LUXURIES)

■ PEARLS FOR THE PALATE: CHOOSING CAVIAR

The secret to appreciating caviar may have something to do with the price. The stuff is so expensive that you tend to slow down and savor those tiny sturgeon eggs instead of scarfing them down like the pigs-in-a-blanket on the hors d'oeuvres tray. Indeed, caviar is expensive: It can easily range in price from $15 to more than $50 an ounce, depending on the freshness and the type.

Break out the silver spoon. Even if the sterling isn't polished, take care to serve your caviar properly for optimum impact. Keep the tin of caviar in the refrigerator until fifteen minutes before serving, then place it in a bowl surrounded by crushed ice. Spoon the caviar carefully, since broken eggs can make the caviar taste a bit oily. Don't put out more than you need, since caviar begins to go bad when exposed to the air.

On the side. The caviar can be accompanied by unbuttered toasted triangles (or points) of white bread or unsalted crackers. Though people often do it, purists consider it a culinary faux pas to serve caviar with onion, sour cream, chopped egg, or lemon, since these strong flavors can detract from the taste of the caviar itself. Buy the good stuff and enjoy the flavors unmasked.

Please pass the salt. Are you kidding? Caviar is packed with salt, though the good stuff, labeled "Malossol," is only mildly salted and comes fresh from the refrigerated section of a specialty store. The cheaper caviar sold in shelf-stable jars is often heavily salted, so beware.

For the sophisticated bargain hunter. Broken eggs don't make a very elegant display, so they are often pressed into blocks and sold separately as "caviar jelly." Pressed caviar usually consists of top-grade eggs, so it has a very rich taste—at a fraction of the price of the whole-grain stuff. You won't get to feel the eggs popping in your mouth, but the caviar flavor comes through loud and clear.

Key Lingo

There are three grades of caviar, depending on the location and species of fish providing the eggs. The most prized caviar comes from three species of sturgeon living in the Caspian Sea.

Beluga caviar: *From Beluga sturgeon, this is the largest and most expensive type because it is the rarest. The eggs are black or dark gray and provide a delicate if somewhat bland taste.*

Osetra caviar: *From Osetra sturgeon, these are nearly as big as the Beluga, but the eggs are brown to gold in color and somewhat less expensive. The flavor has been described as "nutty."*

Sevruga caviar: *As you can guess, this comes from Sevruga sturgeon and consists of much smaller grains or eggs. This type of caviar provides the most intense taste, and at the lowest cost of the three.*

Roe: *This is actually the word for fish eggs, but it is used to describe the processed fish eggs from salmon, whitefish, lump-fish, flying fish, carp, and paddlefish as well as others. Roe tends to have a milder flavor and a lower price tag; it is a far less expensive option to the three sturgeon classics.*

■ GOING FOR THE GOLD: BUYING GOLD JEWELRY

Even an expert eye cannot always tell the difference between karat gold jewelry and gold-filled or electroplate pieces. So why should you spend more—a lot more—to buy jewelry bearing the 14k or 18k mark? Because karat jewelry can last almost forever and the others will eventually show signs of wear.

If you want a ring or necklace to wear as a staple in your jewelry wardrobe, go with karat gold. If you're looking at a piece to wear to work or every once in a while, less expensive gold-filled or plated gold may make more sense.

Key Lingo

To know what you're buying, you need to understand the jeweler's lingo. Here's a quick rundown on the basics:

Solid: *Not necessarily pure 24k gold, solid simply means the piece consists of at least 10k gold and that it is solid, not hollow.*

Gold filled *or* **gold overlay:** *This kind of jewelry is made of a base metal (often jeweler's bronze or sterling silver) coated with a relatively thick layer of gold. The amount of karat gold must equal at least one-twentieth of the total weight.*

Gold plate: *This is the same as gold filled, only the amount of karat gold may be less than one-twentieth of the metal weight.*

Gold electroplate: *An electrolytic process of coating jewelry with a layer of karat gold equal to 7 millionths of an inch.*

Vermeil: *This is jewelry made of sterling silver coated with a layer of gold at least 120 millionths of an inch. Vermeil usually uses a high-karat gold, but a thinner layer than either gold filled or gold plate.*

A question of karats. Before rushing to the jewelry store, you'd best learn the basics about gold fineness or purity. Gold is measured in karats based on a scale of 24, with 100 percent gold equaling 24 karats. Since 24k gold is considered too soft for jewelry making, it is usually alloyed or mixed with other metals to strengthen it. The karat mark indicates the ratio of pure gold to other metals; for example, 18k gold is eighteen parts pure gold and six parts other metals.

Shades of gold. The "other metals" and their proportions will dictate the color of the final piece. Yellow gold is mixed with copper and silver; white gold with nickel or palladium, zinc, and copper; green with silver, copper, and zinc; and pink gold with copper.

Mark of quality. Karat gold jewelry is stamped with a karat mark, indicating how much pure gold the jewelry contains. Be wary if the karat mark only appears on the clasp of a bracelet or necklace. It could mean that only the clasp and not the bracelet itself is 14k gold. Look for the karat mark on a loop or tag attached to the chain or clasp.

Purity and price. Whether or not you want 14k or 18k gold depends largely on how much money you have to spend. Jewelry made of 18k gold tends to be a smidgen softer, but both 14k and 18k gold wear well. (Some upscale jewelers only sell 18k wedding bands, for example.) If you put a necklace made of 14k gold next to one made of 18k gold, you can see a slight difference in color—the 18k item being richer or more *gold* in color—but you'll see a significant difference in price, about 20 percent. Some jewelers try to sell 18k as a status symbol; it's up to you to decide how important the jeweler's stamp is to you.

Trivia to Impress Your Friends

Gold is one of the world's densest elements. It's twice as dense as lead. A cube of gold a mere 12 inches per side weighs a backbreaking 1,200 pounds.

Pound per pound. When buying karat gold jewelry you should take into account weight and workmanship. Unless a piece has extraordinary design or workmanship, buy gold by its weight, comparing the price per gram of gold. You might feel a bit silly asking a jeweler to weigh an 18-inch, 14k herringbone necklace for you, but you'll then be able to compare it with the same necklace offered at the store at the mall. You'll be surprised. The same item can vary significantly in weight and price—and the lightweight versions aren't necessarily cheaper.

Finishing touches. Even if the price is right, don't buy if the item hasn't been finished properly. Examine the clasps on necklaces and bracelets to ensure durability and ease of use. Lightweight chains often use a spring ring; heavier chains often use an interlocking catch with a safety lock called a "box lock" or "lobster claw." A barrel clasp, which looks like part of the chain, is used on most rope chains.

Run the piece of jewelry across your lap and see if it snags on the fabric. Keep an eye out for kinks in the links, mismatched clasps, and end caps that are pressed closed rather than soldered. If you shop carefully, you can find quality jewelry at reasonable prices.

How not to treat your gold jewelry. When you put on your bathing suit, take off your gold jewelry. Chlorinated water can pit and discolor the gold, as well as wear down the alloys used in making 14k and 18k gold.

A band of gold, a ring of green. Some unfortunate souls simply can't wear gold jewelry without their skin turning green. According to the World Gold Council in New York, it's not the gold but the other metals the gold is mixed with. These react with the oils of the skin. One option: Try 18k or 22k gold jewelry; it contains smaller quantities of the other reactive metals.

As for the black marks other people get: It's time to clean your jewelry. Wipe off the accumulated gunk and grime with a soft, moist cloth and your skin will return to normal.

■ AVOIDING THE WILTED LOOK: KEEPING FRESH FLOWERS FRESH

After a couple of days in a water-filled vase, most people find their flowers looking a bit tired and droopy. They wait a day or two more, then toss out the cloudy water and wilted buds. But it need not be so. The life expectancy of most flowers is at least a week, and many hearty varieties can live two or three weeks if properly cared for. You don't need to have a botany degree or a green thumb to keep your bouquet looking fresh. Here are a few tips from the pros:

Dying of thirst. As soon as you arrive home with cut flowers, give them a drink. Cut off the ends of the stems while holding them under warm water. Seems like a lot of trouble, but keep in mind that those poor flowers have been eagerly awaiting a swig of water. After the stem is recut, those flowers will suck air if they can't suck water. To a flower, that's like shooting air into a vein, and it will die four or five days faster than it will if properly cut.

Trivia to Impress Your Friends

When it comes to the thorny issue of the cost of red roses at Valentine's Day, it's not just an issue of florists gouging lovers who want to "say it with flowers." At issue is the fact that most flowers bloom twice a year, six months apart. Flowers that blossom in February also show their colors in mid-summer when demand is much lower. You pay top dollar for roses in winter in part because you're subsidizing the cost of the summer crop when the flowers are not in great demand.

Use surgical precision when cutting a stem. Well, you may not need a scalpel, but you do need either a knife or sharp scissors. Make a clean cut; if you crush the stem by using a blunt instrument, the flower can't suck up the water. Have you ever tried drinking through a crushed straw?

Know the right angle. Make a slant cut on the stem if you wish, but it's not necessary. Time was people thought that a flower wouldn't get enough water if it had a flat cut then stood directly on the bottom of the vase, but florists now know that most flowers drink through their stems as well as the cut on the bottom.

Would you want to drink dirty water? I don't think so. Neither do your flowers. Change the water every day or two. At the same time, wipe down the stems. When they start to feel slimy, it means they're covered with bacteria, which will cause them to break down and clog the stem and lead to a premature death. By merely wiping the stems off under water every couple of days, you can save your flowers from an untimely demise.

More Trivia to Impress Your Friends

To a florist or trivia buff, virtually every flower has a different "meaning." For example, sending purple hyacinth is a way of saying "I'm sorry; please forgive me," and a delivery of viscaria might be a shy suitor's way of asking, "Will you dance with me?" Of course, we all know that red roses mean "I love you," but most of us fail to appreciate the significance of a gift of dried white roses ("Death is preferable to loss of virtue"). Most people welcome the gift of flowers as a thoughtful gesture, but for the more elaborate messages, you probably need to attach a greeting card.

Don't buy dead flowers. Don't laugh; a lot of people do. Plenty of people stand in line at the grocery store and put down good money for floral corpses. How to tell: Look for flowers that haven't germinated. If you can see the pollen—a powdery dust in the middle of the flower—then the flower is on its death bed. Say goodbye and pick another bunch.

Nip it in the bud(s). If you pick a flower with one or more buds on the sides, pinch off their little heads if you want the main flower to grow large or to live longer.

Leave the leaves above water. Go ahead and pluck the leaves below the water line. If you don't, the submerged foliage will break down and cloud the water and clog the stem. Don't go wild and chop them all off, since flowers "exhale," if you will, through the underside of their leaves.

Overcome the wilted look. If flowers droop and wilt, fill the sink with warm water and recut the stems under water. Submerge the flower and leave them covered for about forty-five minutes. This water treatment should spruce them up for a few more days.

That's Bull

Most florists provide a little packet of floral preservative with a delivery of fresh flowers. Use it because it's free, but don't waste your money on the stuff you have to buy yourself. This so-called preservative doesn't preserve the flowers at all; it simply minimizes the growth of bacteria in the water. Forget adding sugar, 7-Up, or aspirin to the water; these don't do any good (unless your flowers have a headache). If you want to fight the slime of bacterial buildup in the water, all you need to do is add about a half teaspoon of Clorox bleach to every gallon of water to kill the bacteria.

■ STERLING QUALITIES: SELECTING SILVER

Sterling silver isn't a second-place metal. Though it's much less expensive than gold or platinum, this precious metal makes breathtaking jewelry, flatware, and gift items. In order to be stamped "sterling," an item must contain 92.5 percent pure silver and 7.5 percent of an alloy such as copper, which is added for strength. (Pure silver is too soft to be used alone.) A piece of sterling may also be stamped ".925," indicating its purity.

Not quite pure. Outside the United States, some silver items contain more alloys and less silver. These metals may look less white and gleaming to the well-trained eye, but an unsuspecting American tourist may not be able to tell without checking the stamp. Some inferior metals will be marked .875 or even .750.

Key Lingo

Hollowware: *This refers to large hollow objects such as bowls, pitchers, serving dishes, candlesticks, and trays that are made of either solid sterling or silver plate.*

Nickel silver: *This isn't silver at all. It's actually an alloy of nickel, copper, and zinc with a drop of silver in it.*

Patina: *This refers to the soft luster caused by tiny scratches in silver that come from frequent use.*

Silver plate: *This is the process of electroplating sterling silver over a base metal, usually an alloy of nickel, copper, or brass.*

Solid silver: *This refers to an object that isn't hollow and is made of sterling silver.*

Tarnished by time. When exposed to the air, silver will react or oxidize and develop a thin layer of black tarnish. The metal doesn't break down in the same way that iron rusts; the film can easily be removed with a commercial silver polish or with some hot soapy water and elbow grease.

Trivia to Impress Your Friends

Silver is so malleable that it can be hammered into sheets so thin that it would take 100,000 of them to make a stack an inch high.

When is sterling really stainless? When it's the blade of a sterling silver knife. Almost all the knives in sterling silver flatware sets consist of stainless steel blades. The stainless can be made sharper and more durable, and once it is polished and attached to the sterling silver handle, it's difficult to tell the piece is not entirely made of sterling.

More Trivia to Impress Different Friends

In the twelfth century, five towns in eastern Germany banded together to trade with England. In exchange for English cattle and grain, the group traded its own currency, silver coins called "Easterlings." The silver coins, known and respected for their purity, became the basis for the English coin. Over time, the name was shortened to "sterling," and later borrowed to refer to the pure silver metal.

■ HARD CHOICES: PICKING A DIAMOND

Diamonds are magic. They have become such powerful symbols of romance and prestige that no other gemstone sends quite the same message. Some ancient Greeks called diamonds splinters of stars; others referred to them as the tears of the Gods. Diamonds have been used to drive away evil spirits, to induce sexual prowess, and, of course, to declare undying devotion between lovers.

Buying the right diamond is one part passion, two parts research. Like snowflakes, every diamond is unique, but there are four factors to consider when assessing a diamond's value: carat weight, color, clarity, and cut.

Not your garden-variety carats. Diamonds are measured by the carat, a unit of measure equal to one-fifth of a gram, meaning there are 142 carats to an ounce. Carats are further broken into points; one carat equals 100 points. A 53-point diamond would be slightly over half a carat. If you're able to afford a diamond in the one-carat range, be sure to choose one that is at least one full carat. Those slightly less—.96 or .98 carats, for example—are considerably less valuable than a full-carat stone.

Across the spectrum. Diamonds can be any color, but most of the finest stones are white. White diamonds are graded from D to Z (colorless to cloudy yellow), with the stones closest to icy white being the most valuable. With colored diamonds, known as "fancies," the stones are judged by their depth of color. The Hope Diamond is blue, and the Tiffany Diamond is canary red.

Trivia to Impress Your Friends

The largest diamond ever found is the Cullinan, which weighed in at an amazing 3,106 carats—or slightly less than 1 1/2 pounds!

Nobody's perfect. And neither is a diamond. A diamond considered "flawless" simply has no imperfections visible under a microscope that magnifies ten times. A stone's clarity takes into account the number, size, and location of any "inclusions" or irregularities in a diamond. Sometimes referred to as "nature's birthmarks," spots, bubbles, lines, and other imperfections were formed in the stone when it was created from carbon millions of years ago.

A cut above. The cut is more than a matter of personal preference. No matter what the shape, the depth and symmetry of the stone should be in proper proportion in order to maximize the stone's brilliance or "fire." If the stone is cut too deep or too shallow, the light will escape before being reflected from facet to facet and back through the top of the stone. Diamonds are cut following an exact mathematical formula, with 58 facets or flat planes cut into each stone.

What price beauty? Because there are so many variables, it's almost impossible to generalize on diamond prices. For example, you could spend $3,000 or $10,000 for a 1-carat diamond. The less expensive diamond might have some flaws, or its color might not be good, or the stone may not be cut well. Some people shop for diamond quality, others for quantity or size. No two diamonds are alike; it's up to you to decide how much you're willing to spend and how important quality is to you.

What a rock. When buying a diamond, base your decision on the quality and value of the stone, not the setting. Mounting the stone is a matter of personal taste and preference. Even if you're comparing two pieces of mounted jewelry, find out the carat weight, clarity, color, and cut of each stone and consider that separately.

That's Bull

Don't buy diamond jewelry as an investment; buy it because you want to wear and enjoy it. Why? Diamonds you'll buy at retail have been marked up by about 100 percent. If you needed to sell a diamond, you'd probably find it worth only about 20 percent of the appraised replacement cost. Diamonds do appreciate in value, but usually not enough to offset the markup. Keep making those deposits in your retirement account.

■ CULTURED JEWELS:
BUYING PEARL JEWELRY

No single piece of fine jewelry says "class" like a simple strand of cultured pearls. Not flashy like diamonds or colored gemstones, pearls offer a more subtle luster and soothing beauty. Pearls can be dressed up or down; they can be worn to work or to the most formal occasion. Whether you're considering a fourteen-inch choker or a thirty-six-inch opera-length strand, buying pearls requires a basic understanding of quality and fashion options.

Jewels of the sea. Pearls form inside oysters after a piece of sand or shell gets stuck inside the shell. To protect against the irritant, the oyster secretes a smooth, crystalline substance known as nacre. Layer after layer of nacre builds up, until after several years, a pearl is born.

Lending Mother Nature a hand. Cultured pearls are formed in the same way as natural pearls, only the irritant is placed into the oyster rather than waiting for it to happen by accident. These oysters are then raised on "pearl farms" in protected waters. Despite the attempts to control Mother Nature, only about 3 to 5 percent of the oysters go on to produce pearls good enough for use in jewelry. The only way to tell the difference between a natural and cultured pearl is by X-ray.

Pearls of great price. Prices vary greatly from pearl to pearl, depending on the luster, size, shape, and type of pearl. You can buy a decent sixteen-inch strand for $350, or you can spend as much as $75,000 for a fourteen-inch strand of fifteen-millimeter Burmese sea pearls.

Key Lingo

Cultured pearls are grown in waters around the world, but oysters work their magic differently depending on local conditions. The result: a number of distinct types of pearls.

Akoya pearls: These grow in the Akoya oyster off the coast of Japan. Known for their luster and fine grain, they are the most common saltwater pearls sold, accounting for 85 percent of the total. They range in size from two to 10 millimeters.

Burmese pearls: Grown in Burma, these are among the largest —and most expensive—pearls grown. They are known for their pinkish cast and grainy surface, as well as their size, which can range from 10 to 17 millimeters.

Freshwater pearls: Flat and elongated, freshwater pearls grow in mollusks, not oysters, that live in lakes and streams. Chinese freshwater pearls, the most common type, come from mainland China. Biwa freshwater pearls grow in Japan's Lake Biwa and tend to be smoother and more lustrous than the Chinese version. They are much less expensive than round, saltwater pearls.

Keshi pearls: These are tiny seed pearls that form in cultivated oysters.

Mabe pearls: Not round, they look a bit like a pearl that has melted slightly. Formed against the oyster's shell instead of within the oyster's flesh, their shape is more conducive to being mounted in jewelry rather than strung as beads. They are grown in western Japan, Australia, and the Philippines, and range in size from 10 to 15 millimeters across.

South Sea pearls: These come from the South Sea oyster in the Southwest Pacific, off the coast of Australia. They are a lot like Burmese pearls, only they have a silvery sheen and often cost somewhat (but not much) less. Their size ranges from 10 to 17 millimeters.

The bigger, the better. Or at least the more expensive. In addition to size, look for pearls with deep sheen or luster, even color, and good symmetry. If you're buying a strand of pearls, make sure the individual pearls are blended by size and color. Test the strand by rolling it across a flat surface; any pearls that haven't been drilled properly will wiggle as they roll.

If you wear dentures, forget it. If not, then you can test whether a pearl is real by rubbing it against your teeth. The surface of a pearl should appear satiny, but it may look irregular up close. These natural irregularities will cause a real pearl to feel gritty when you run it across the surface of your teeth.

All tied up in knots. In this case, that's good. A strand of pearls should have knots between each pearl so they won't scatter and be lost if the silk string breaks. The tiny knots also keep the pearls from rubbing against one another and causing scratches.

To know me is to love me. And to love your pearls is to wear and enjoy them. Pearls are organic gems that need contact with your body's oils to keep them satiny and vital. Pearls stored in dry, stuffy bank vaults for years on end can lose their luster.

Diamonds are the tough gems. Pearls are delicate and deserve to be treated with respect. You should store pearls in a chamois bag or wrapped in tissue paper to avoid scratches. Perfume, makeup, and hairspray can damage pearls, so you should be dressed and ready to head out the door before donning your jewelry. Of course, pearls should be cleaned with mild soap and water rather than with chemicals or abrasives.

■ BUYING A FUR TO BRING OUT THE BEAST IN YOU

If you find faux furs a fashion faux pas and you don't mind being "politically incorrect," then you may want to wrap yourself in a plush, luxurious fur coat. These days you can get a decent mink for about $5,000—or you can spend as much as $50,000 for a one-of-a-kind chinchilla coat. So what's the difference between the two? Ultimately, the price of a fur coat depends on the number and quality of skins and the overall workmanship. Lousy finishing and poor design can make a coat of the finest mink look like it was made out of second-rate muskrat.

I wouldn't know a mink if it came up and bit me. Before buying a coat, get to know your pelts. Start by trying on the best garment in the fur of your choice. This top-of-the-line coat will show you how the best pelts look and feel (and it will be fun, too). Out of your price range? That's OK. Enjoy the coat and let your fingers "learn" the fur. In no time you'll figure out how to "feel your way" and weed out inferior pelts. You'll want to compare both the quality of the fur and the design of the coat. Sometimes choosing a simpler sleeve or a more streamlined collar can bring the cost down considerably.

Sexual discrimination encouraged. But only when it comes to comparing furs. With some furs—including mink, sable, and lynx—female skins are more expensive than male skins, because they are smaller, lighter, and more flexible. If an all-female coat exceeds your fur-buying budget, consider a "male" coat with "female" sleeves—a sort of fashion hermaphrodite. You can usually save about $1,000 and you'll appreciate the more relaxed, supple fur in the sleeves most of all.

Key Lingo

Grooving: *The method of shearing fur in "stripes" of different widths and depths.*

Grotzen: *The thick, coarse hair along the center of a pelt.*

Guard hair: *Long, lustrous outer hair that protects the underfur.*

Plucking: *Removing coarse guard hairs to emphasize the beauty of the fur. All guard hairs are plucked before shearing.*

Ranch raised: *Most furs are now raised on ranches the same way cattle, sheep, and other animals are raised for food.*

Shearing: *Cutting fur to a short, uniform pile.*

Tip-dyeing (or blending): *Applying dye to the tips of the guard hairs to produce more uniformity in color.*

Underfur: *The underhair covered by guard hairs.*

The animal wore it every day. True, but that doesn't mean you can. Some furs—such as mink, raccoon, and beaver—are tough enough to stand up for all-around wear. Others—such as broadtail, mole, and lynx—tend to be more fragile and may need to be saved for special-occasion wear.

If Mother Nature intended furs to be purple, she would have made them that way. But Mother Nature didn't have access to the high-tech bleaching and dyeing processes we have today. In general, skip the funky colors on a fur you want to wear for years and years; the dyes will eventually oxidize and alter the color in unpredictable ways. A lousy dye job can also cause the skins to crack and split more readily.

Have you ever seen a mink wear lipstick? They never use the stuff. Makeup on the collar will discolor a fur. Of course, it feels good to snuggle into a fur collar, but wear a neck scarf unless your fur exactly matches your foundation color. Also, douse yourself with perfume and cologne before putting on your coat, not after; the oils and alcohol can damage the pelts. While you're at it, avoid chain belts and heavy jewelry that will rub the fur and damage the hairs, and forgo the temptation to pin corsages, flowers, and jewelry to the lapels.

Hey, honey, look what the cat dragged in. If you and your coat look a little soggy and matted after being caught in a rainstorm, shake off the fur and hang it on a large wooden hanger away from heat in an area where the air circulates freely. After it's dry, shake it out again. Never, never, never use an electric blow dryer on a fur. Likewise, skip the brushing and combing routines.

You're the second one to wear this fur. How about a third? When shopping for a secondhand fur, look for the same signs of quality—for a fraction of the cost. You'll know a fur is secondhand because the label must say so under federal law. The law also requires that the label on any fur selling for more than $5 reveal the name of the fur and whether the natural texture has been altered by shearing, dyeing, or tip-dyeing.

Bargains north of the border. It's cold up there in Canada. Furriers in Montreal, the center of Canada's fur industry, sell a lot more fur per capita than in the good old U.S. of A. What does that mean for you? Savings of about $2,500 to $3,000.

Not for New Yorkers only. Not heading to Montreal any time soon? How about the Big Apple? You can get a bargain on an American-made fur from the wholesalers in New York's fur district (around Seventh Avenue and 30th Street in Manhattan). Typical savings: about 30 to 40 percent below retail. Just because the prices are apt to be lower doesn't mean you can get by without doing your homework; you still need to shop around to make sure you're getting good value instead of just a low price.

What to do when it's time to shed your fur. All good things must come to an end. When those first crocuses push up signaling the first signs of spring, it's time to check into leaving your fur in a furrier's vault. Don't be foolish and stash it in a cedar or mothball-infested closet wrapped in plastic. This is a surefire way to dry the skin and rot the silk lining.

■ BEYOND PAPER PLATES: BUYING DINNERWARE

Elegant dining consists of more than elegant fare; it requires proper presentation on high-quality china. There are several types of fine and casual dinnerware. Except for differences in formula and decoration, the production process is similar for all the different types.

To make fine china, refined clays, feldspar, flint, and other ingredients are ground into a fine powder, then mixed with enough water to make a mixture similar in texture to heavy cream. This concoction, called slip, is cast in molds, shaped, and fired in giant kilns, often at temperatures high enough to melt many metals. During the firing, the particles in the plate melt and fuse together. The piece is then glazed, refired, and ready for decoration.

To a large degree, the differences in decoration determine price. You can spend as little as $50 for a five-piece place setting of simple china, or as much as $250 for fine bone china trimmed in 14-karat gold or platinum.

Casual dinnerware, such as ironstone and earthenware, is similar but made of thick, opaque clays that cannot take the extreme heat used for fine china. This type of dinnerware tends to be heavier, so it is better able to withstand frequent use and family dinners. It also costs a lot less, but the rule about decoration still applies. You can choose a plain pattern that costs $20 or $30 a setting, or a hand-painted design that costs $75 to $100.

Is that Avon calling? No, it's your fine china declaring that it's the real thing. Like crystal, a fine china plate will sound a bell-like ring when struck with a pencil or tapped with a fingernail.

Key Lingo

When shopping for china, don't be confused by the various terms and processes described in the literature. Here's a quick rundown on what's what in the china cabinet:

Belleck: *An ivory-colored porcelain with an iridescent glaze, produced in Belleck, Ireland.*

Bisque or biscuit ware: *A piece of ware that has gone through the first firing but has not yet been glazed.*

Bone china: *Fine china that contains bone ash (or an equivalent substance), which gives bone china both its whiteness and its name.*

Earthenware: *Thick, opaque, and porous ware made from clays that can't tolerate the extreme heat used to make fine china.*

Fine china: *A translucent and nonporous china; the ingredients in the clays have been heated to such high temperatures that they have melted and bonded together. Fine china is stronger and thinner than other types of dinnerware.*

Ironstone: *A heavy earthenware.*

Stoneware: *A nonporous ware that is not translucent; it's stronger than regular earthenware but not as strong as ironstone.*

They still look like new. That's because you store your dinnerware properly between use. Don't stack the pieces one on top of another to the top shelf of your cabinet. If you have a delicate decoration, put a layer of felt or bubblewrap between the plates. Hang cups separately or stack them two by two.

Just do it. Use the good stuff. Life is too short to reserve your fine china only for holidays. Of course, it's usually not practical to use the delicate china on a day-to-day basis, but don't wait for the twice-a-year celebrations to enjoy the regal dining experience of eating from your best dinnerware.

Stock up. Or, if you can't afford to buy the entire service for twelve at one time, do it a setting at a time by choosing a pattern with open stock. Not only can you collect pieces over time, with open stock a shattered dinner plate or chipped saucer isn't such a big deal since it can easily be replaced.

Second best . . . But still good enough. If you have access to a factory outlet or discount mall, check out the factory seconds. These items usually have some kind of flaw —some minor, some quite noticeable—but you can have them for a deep discount, often half the regular price. Be sure to check the items over carefully, you know there's a problem somewhere.

■ SECOND CHANCES: FINDING ANTIQUES

Unless you know the business, the secret to buying antiques is finding a fair and honest shopkeeper. At the most basic level, the value of an antique depends on its age—usually a hundred years or older—its condition, and whether or not the item is still being made. For example, a silver pattern that is no longer made is worth more than one that is still available.

Can I get that in writing? When you make a purchase, ask the antiques dealer to describe in writing on the receipt exactly what it is that you're buying. Don't accept a note that simply says "wooden chair." What style? Is it an original or a reproduction? What year (approximately) was it made? Has it been altered or repaired? If a dispute later arises about whether the item sold to you is what was represented, your receipt will be the only proof of what you were told at the time of purchase.

I kept stubbing my toe on the dresser. Sounds like a good reason not to buy a piece of furniture, but you wouldn't know that a piece of furniture might crowd the room until you take it home for a weekend. Before you buy a large piece of furniture or other antique, ask if you can take it home on approval before you finalize the purchase. Be sure to get this in writing, so that you won't get stuck with something that doesn't fit or doesn't look right in the place you had envisioned.

That's Bull

Some antiques dealers provide appraisals that show you'll be paying a fair price—or even getting a great deal—on an item available for sale in the shop. You might think you can put your money down and not look back, but don't fall for this trick. Often what you will receive is a retail appraisal price (what you would expect to pay at a retail store) not the fair market value (which is what you would get for the item if you tried to sell it yourself).

There are more fish in the sea. And more antiques to discover. You'll find the best goods at the best price if you're willing to take the time to comparison shop. Before walking into the shop, know what you want to buy—and what you want to pay. If you're new to antiquing, take a look at some antique auction catalogs and magazines to find out what you like and how much you might expect to pay. Then browse the books available at the public library and look at price guides for more information. The more you know, the less you'll depend on luck to get what you want at an affordable price.

Be sure to snoop. Give your antiques a careful examination before you buy. Go through all the drawers and make sure they glide smoothly. Check tables for structural stability. Look for scratches, chips, and broken pieces. Many auction houses or antiques dealers can recommend cabinetmakers who specialize in antiques and can tell you how long it should take to do the necessary repairs.

More Bull

Well-meaning friends and even some antiques dealers may suggest you go to an estate sale to find a bargain on something you're looking for. But an estate sale is not a fancy name for a garage sale, and items may be priced higher than they would be at an antiques shop because bargain-hunters are going to assume that they're going to get a good deal. You've got to know the value of what you're buying; if you're going to rely on the seller to offer you a great deal, then you're going to overpay. Be careful: When you buy from an estate sale, all sales are final. Period.

Auto dealers allow trade-ins. And so do some antiques dealers. If you buy a piece of furniture from a shop and later decide you'd like to upgrade to a more expensive item, many shops will give you credit for the amount you paid on the first item, provided it's still in the same condition.

Cheaper by the dozen—and by the inch. Very large antiques often sell at low prices because few people have enough room to accommodate them. Similarly, tall chests usually cost less than low ones because people can't hang pictures above them. If you've got the room, bigger can mean bigger bargains.

You're not getting older, you're getting better. And so is a lot of the stuff that's collecting dust in your attic and garage. If you're ready to get rid of these antiques, you might want to offer them on consignment at a local shop. The dealer sets the price and collects about 25 to 30 percent of the sales price and you pocket the rest. (The normal markup on antiques is 100 percent.) You'll get more money offering something for sale on consignment than you would if the dealer bought the item outright, but you won't get the money until the item is sold, which could be a long time —or never.

Ain't nothin' like the real thing, baby. In many cases antiques are cheaper and better investments than modern reproductions. You might be asked to pay $5,000 for a modern reproduction of a Georgian mahogany bow-front chest, even though the originals can be found at auction for around $1,000. Furthermore, that reproduction piece is going to be "used furniture" as soon as you buy it (and it will be worth only about one-third the price you paid), but the "antique" will retain its value over time.

Don't Forget to Ask

☐ *How long have you been in business?*
☐ *How long have you been at this location?*
☐ *Do you have any references?*
☐ *Has this piece been repaired or altered?*
☐ *If so, were the repairs done well?*
☐ *Can I return this piece if it doesn't fit in my home?*

■ WHAT'S IT WORTH TO YOU?
BUYING AT AUCTIONS

If you think fast and can listen even faster, then you might be able to find a bargain—or at least a good deal—at an auction house or on-site estate-sale auction. Whether it's antiques, horses, or farm equipment on the auction block, most auctions work the same way: You register with a clerk, who takes down your name, address, and some identification and gives you a numbered bidder card. At the start of the auction, the auctioneer reads off the terms of the auction, then launches into the fast-talking "chant" and the bidding begins.

Caveat emptor, caveat emptor. Again, caveat emptor. Need I say more? Take time to preview all the items included in the auction. Open all the drawers, examine every square inch of the item for chips, cracks, tears, stains, and missing pieces. A good auctioneer will point out any flaws, but it's up to you to examine the goods before you bid. Every item is sold "as is," so you'll get no sympathy if you complain to the auctioneer that the vase you just bought has a crack in it. In fact, what you're apt to hear is, "We won't charge extra for the crack."

Bring the U-Haul. The terms of sale are actually "as is/where is," meaning it's up to you to haul away your new purchases after you buy them. Some facilities will make special arrangements if you buy a large item, but for the most part you better be ready to take it all with you when you go.

Trivia to Impress Your Friends

An embarrassing bit of auction history: Auctions have their roots in ancient Babylonian marriage markets, where the price for a young woman started high and was lowered until a "taker" accepted the price.

The sky is the limit. But you should have a ceiling. The auctioneer will do everything he or she can to bring on "the fever"; it's your job to stay cool. Make a budget of what you're willing to spend on every item you plan to bid on. When the price exceeds your budget, put your bid card down. Resist temptation . . . and come back again next week and try again.

Keep your eyes open. Go to a couple of auctions in your area and you'll have no trouble figuring out who the antiques dealers are. If you want to be sure to get a good price, learn to take cues from them. Most antiques dealers don't overbid; they know the market price for certain items and they know what they want to take home for dealer markup. When the dealers drop out of the bidding, the price may be getting too high.

When the weather is bad, the bidding is good.

Rain, snow, sleet, excessive heat—these are the conditions you seek when attending auctions. It won't be much fun to go out in the foul weather, but some of your competition may stay home, leaving the bargains to you. Another good time: Weekends when there are craft fairs and other activities that will draw crowds away from the auctions.

Bid early, bid late. It's up to the auctioneer to "stack" the goods or determine the order of sale. Some will put the best items early, others wait until the end. One rule generally applies, a few sacrificial lambs go up on the auction block to get the crowd warmed up before the good stuff comes out. People often get the best prices on the early items, when bidders are just getting into the spirit of the occasion, and at the end of the day, when the crowd has thinned and most of the people still there have already spent their money.

■ KEYS TO PICKING A PIANO

Before you get to Carnegie Hall, you'll have to practice, practice, practice—at home. Practice can be a pleasure with the right instrument. The richest sounds come from the eighty-eight keys on a nine-foot concert grand piano, but they can cost a bundle and take up a lot of elbow room. Smaller upright models or downsized baby grands fit more readily in most people's budgets—and living rooms.

A grand piano is about five feet wide and between four and a half and nine and a half feet long; a vertical piano is about five feet wide and about two to two and a half feet deep. Then add to both measurements about two feet for the piano bench and the person sitting on it.

Don't judge a book by its cover. But pay careful

attention to a piano's case. Don't expect to find a solid thickness of wood. The case should consist of a softwood base, covered with several layers of hardwood veneer, such as oak, maple, walnut, and mahogany. Finished properly, the grains of the hardwood veneers run in different directions, improving on Mother Nature by protecting against splits or chips in the case wood. Ask if cheaper materials, such as plywood, plastic, or compressed sawdust, have been substituted anywhere in the case; sometimes the quality of the case helps explain significant differences in the final cost of a piano.

Key Lingo

Size does matter, and don't let anyone tell you otherwise. The best sound comes from grand pianos, which are constructed on a horizontal plane, with their strings stretched horizontally across the piano plate and framework. Upright or vertical pianos are constructed on a vertical plane, with their strings stretched vertically across the piano plate and framework. In general, the horizontal configuration allows the sound to develop more fully; uprights sometimes make the music sound boxed in. Pianos are often referred to by size:

Concert grand: *7½ to 9½ feet long*

Medium grand: *5½ to 7½ feet long*

Baby grand: *4½ to 5½ feet long*

Full-size upright: *49 to 60 inches high*

Studio: *45 to 48 inches high*

Console: *40 to 43 inches high*

Spinet: *35 to 39 inches high*

Don't get carried away by differences of an inch or two, which can reflect nothing more than an extra thick lid or larger casters. Instead, compare the inside scale design.

Finishing touches matter. Sure they're all smooth and unblemished, but they won't all stay that way. Piano cases can be glossy or matte, painted or natural wood. The type of case you choose is a matter of personal preference, but you should probably steer clear of glossy finishes if you have children at home, since polished finishes highlight scratches. Whatever finish you choose, keep it clean and polished; all finishes will dry out and crack if not properly treated. If you choose a lacquered finish, be sure the piano has at least three coats.

Stay tuned. Every six months you should do two things: visit your dentist and get your piano tuned. The overall pitch of a piano changes with variations in humidity and temperature. Even if your new piano was in tune at the store when you bought it, you should have it tuned again three to six weeks after it has settled into your home. If the piano wasn't in good pitch and tune at the store, it should be pitched and tuned at the time of delivery, and then again three to six weeks later. Keeping your piano tuned will both increase your enjoyment of the instrument and lengthen the instrument's life: Pianos tuned infrequently deteriorate tonally and mechanically at least twice as fast as pianos that have been properly maintained.

Picky, picky, picky. Keep in mind that a piano is a delicate instrument: It needs a cool, dry room away from direct sunlight and not too close to radiators or air-conditioner vents. Don't jam your piano into a tiny corner —it needs to be positioned at least four inches away from the wall to allow the sound to resonate without sounding muffled.

Alive with the sound of music. For this you can thank the hefty gray cast-iron metal plate at the heart of your piano. This enormous plate is required to withstand the enormous overall tension of the nearly 230 strings in a typical piano. When stretched to the assigned pitch, these strings exert a pull equal to 16 to 23 tons, depending on the size of the piano. The metal plates not only resist the tension without signs of fatigue, but they also absorb the vibration without ringing or transferring the sound. Not all plates do their work equally well: They all try to achieve the highest possible safety margin over the strength necessary to support the strings, but they vary greatly in thickness, weight, and design. The stronger the plate, the longer the piano will stay in tune. Ask the dealer about the safety margins of the iron plates in the various models you are considering.

Put the lid down when you're finished. Or, in this case, before you start. Unless you live in a concert hall or recording studio, chances are the acoustics in your home are less than grand. Many dealers encourage you to try their instruments in showrooms designed to enhance the sound —hardwood floors, sparse furnishings, the piano lid up. Sure, the piano will sound fabulous under these circumstances, but it may not perform quite as well in your living room. When it's time for you to take a test run at the keyboard, put the lid down to get a bit better idea of how the instrument might sound at home.

Tickling the plastics. Truth-in-advertising demands this expression be used, since pianos made today have plastic key covers instead of the legendary ivory. Serious pianists often prefer ivory keys because they absorb sweat and don't get slippery, but ivory importation is illegal because it requires killing the elephants for their tusks. Alas, pianists need not choose between their passion for music and their love of Dumbo and Babar; manufacturers are now hard at work in their laboratories developing synthetic keyboard materials that feel just like ivory.

A sound investment. Before settling on a piano, shop around. Prices can vary widely, depending on size, brand, and dealer. You should be able to find a decent new vertical piano for $3,000 and up, or a new grand for $7,000 and up—way up. (Some top-of-the-line models can cost as much as luxury cars.) Steinway sets the standard; you'll pay more for a Steinway, but they often bring more in resales compared to other brands in comparable condition. Baldwin, Mason & Hamlin, and Knabe also make good pianos, as do the Japanese manufacturers Yamaha and Kawai.

They just don't make 'em like they used to. Some old pianos have exquisite veneers, cases, leg styles, and ivory keys that you can't find on new models (unless you're willing to take out a second mortgage on the house). Since the average life of a piano is around fifty years (and with proper restoration fifty more), you might want to check into the used piano market before buying.

Used grands usually cost from three to six times as much as vertical pianos of similar quality and condition. For example, a used upright might cost $300 to $800; a used grand $1,000 to $5,000. Certain "brand names," such as Steinway, will demand a higher price. Buy the best piano you can afford, without compromising quality. If you can't afford a high-quality grand piano, then don't settle for a cheap used one or you'll find yourself with a large piece of furniture that sounds terrible when you play it. (Your friends might not know better and assume that you're a lousy piano player instead of rightfully blaming the instrument.)

Over twenty and over the hill. Used pianos may be on the market at low prices, but in general it doesn't make sense to buy one that's much over ten years old—and almost never over twenty—unless it has been restored, of course. When shopping for a used model, have a piano tuner check it out before putting any money down. You wouldn't buy a used car without a mechanic's input, would you? Unless you're a pro, make sure someone who knows pianos can guarantee that it's ready to make beautiful music with you.

The bionic piano. When comparing used pianos, beware what is meant by various states of repair. In general, repair means fixing broken parts, period. Reconditioning means upgrading the piano, but with as little replacement of parts as possible. For example, in addition to a thorough cleaning, the hammers may be resurfaced (instead of being replaced). Repairing means replacing parts—restringing and replacing the pinblock, as well as many other parts—enough to put it into ''factory new'' condition.

When is a bargain not a bargain? When it's not really for sale. Piano dealers often offer used pianos as bait to lure customers into their stores, then they try to push the new, more expensive models. In many cases, these used models are overpriced and out of tune so that no one will want to buy them in the first place. You also need to be wary of used pianos offered for sale by private owners, who tend to think their instruments are in better condition and worth more money than they really are. If you're definitely in the market for a used piano, you're apt to have the best luck buying from a professional piano repair and rebuilding shop.

Not worth the paper it's printed on. Some manufacturers try to use warranties as yet another sales gimmick. Read the fine print: Some warranties require that you pay to ship the piano back to the dealer if it can't be fixed at your home; others don't cover the finish, or require that you show proof you have had the instrument tuned at the recommended intervals (even though most defects won't be related to whether the piano has been tuned). A parts-only warranty is virtually worthless without the labor contract to go with it.

That's Bull

Some piano dealers and manufacturers try to impress prospective
buyers by highlighting the number and thickness of the support
posts in the piano back. These posts are supposed to avoid
excess weight by increasing the load on the piano back and
decreasing the tension on the metal plate. Sure the piano is
lighter—it has less metal and more wood in it—but that
doesn't necessarily make it better. Don't judge the piano's
overall strength by counting the back posts; some manufactur-
ers actually nail in a few extras for show. The weight is a
more accurate measure of structural strength, since it probably
reflects a heavier, stronger metal piano plate. In general, the
lighter the piano, the higher the tuning and upkeep costs.
The average spinet or console weighs in at from 300 to 500
pounds, full-size uprights at 700 to 1,000 pounds; grands
vary from 500 to 1,000, though a concert grand can weigh
in at a whopping 1,300 pounds.

■ THE REAL THING: BUYING GENUINE LEATHER

These days it can be quite tricky to tell real leather from the
man-made vinyl look-alikes. On the shelf, a good imitation
leather can appear virtually identical to its natural cousin,
but when it comes to long-term wear, the real leather still
stands apart in terms of durability and performance.

Accept no substitutes. Leather is strong. It can have
a tensile strength of up to 5,000 pounds per square inch,
which makes sense considering that it used to hold a cow or

some other large animal together. Leather can be identified by its irregular pattern, surface blemishes, lack of color uniformity, variation in thickness, and variations in grain.

The animal had a snug fit. But if you buy a leather garment too tight, it may shrink and be unwearable. Hides are stretched during tanning and some relaxation shrinkage can be expected in use and cleaning.

Have you ever seen a purple cow? Though the color leather you choose is largely based on fashion and taste, given the option choose lighter colors. These products are less likely to fade and cause dye transfer during cleaning.

A new look. After cleaning, a leather garment may not look the same as it did before. Certain defects in the hide can appear during the cleaning process. For example, the animal may have been injured by briars, barbed wire, disease, or fights. The scar tissue doesn't dye evenly, so it is covered with fillers before dyeing. Hides that are so thick that they are split can reveal veins that show up as irregular wavy lines. These defects may be masked with fillers and dyes but show up after cleaning.

Wrinkles come with age. Skins taken from the neck or belly of an animal are naturally wrinkled. They are stretched during manufacturing, but the skin will relax with age and the wrinkles can reappear. Learn to accept wrinkles on yourself—and your leather goods.

Key Lingo

Leather goods must be labeled with the composition of the hide. The following terms are often used in the descriptions:

Leather: *The basic term for a hide or skin that has been tanned, but the original structure has been left more or less intact. The animal's hair or wool may or may not have been removed.*

Grain: _The pattern left on the outer surface of the hide after the animal's hair or wool has been removed._

Grain split: _The outermost layer of a thick hide that has been separated into two or more layers._

Top grain or full grain: _Leather that has not had the surface grain altered in any way, except that the hair or wool may have been removed. This is the only type of hide that can be called "genuine leather." It is the strongest, wears the best, and takes finishing better than other leathers._

Corrected grain: _Leather that has had the grain removed or altered by sanding or buffing._

Split leather: _The leather layer left behind when the grain split (top layer) has been removed. This flesh or middle layer is often used to make suede leather. It can also be treated to simulate the color and grain of top grain. Goods made of split leather are usually less expensive than those made of top grain._

Suede: _Leather with a velvetlike nap created by sanding or buffing the leather surface to separate the fibers._

Crust: _Sometimes called "naked leather," the crust is leather that has been tanned, dyed, and dried but not finished._

Embossed: _Leather that has been pressed or printed to reveal a raised pattern; some embossing attempts to resemble a type of natural grain, others are strictly ornamental patterns._

Processed leather: _Leather that has been treated to look like another type; for example, calfskin embossed to look like alligator skin._

Bonded leather: _Leather scraps that are pulverized and bonded together with glue._

Chapter Seven

It's the Little
Things
(That Add Up)

■ THE MAGAZINE SUBSCRIPTION PRESCRIPTION

If you receive some of the 12 billion consumer magazines mailed each year in the United States, then you're undoubtedly familiar with the annoying subscription renewal notices publishers begin mailing as soon as you first sign up to receive a magazine. Granted, the magazine needs to get to its subscribers early enough to process their renewals in time to avoid any lapse in service, but the constant bombardment with order forms and offers can be quite a bother.

I surrender, I surrender. At least six months before you're due to receive your final issue, the notices begin. If you plan to renew, do yourself a favor and do so early. Publishers don't want to encourage their subscribers to dillydally (it's expensive for them to send out repeated notices), so with most magazines the offers don't get any cheaper if you wait.

Read from cover to cover, including the mailing label. That's where you can find the code indicating the date of the last issue you have paid for. If you don't trust the publisher to fulfill your subscription in full, then make a note of when your subscription begins and ends, and check your findings against the date listed on the address label. For example: Jan96 means you will continue receiving magazines until January 1996.

You just might get lucky. You don't need to buy a magazine to enter one of the magazine subscription house sweepstakes, but if you do sign up you will be guaranteed the lowest possible price. The way these deals work, Publishers Clearing House or some other subscription service keeps almost all the money generated by your initial subscription; the magazine accepts the loss with the hope that you will enjoy the magazine and renew.

If you're really cheap and want to drive a hard bargain, compare the subscription price offered on your renewal notice with the price listed in the sweepstakes offer. If the renewal offer is higher, agree to renew, but only at the guaranteed-lowest sweepstakes price. (This technique is recommended only for people who like to haggle and have a lot of time on their hands; in most cases the price difference won't amount to more than a dollar or two.)

■ BACK TO THE INKWELL: PURCHASING A PEN

These days we tend to call instead of write, to print it out rather than write it out, to photocopy instead of take notes. Still, despite our dependence on word processors and cheap ballpoint pens, a growing number of people are discovering the pleasure of using distinguished writing instruments. We're not talking about 29-cent Bic ballpoints here.

Buying a pen involves attitude. You might find pleasure in a $30 Sheaffer fountain pen, or you might insist on spending an inconceivable $13,500 on a platinum Montblanc fountain pen with an 18-karat gold tip or "nib." Of course, when you buy a pen with a handcrafted exterior of precious metal you're paying for more than the writing mechanism (let's just hope your words are poetic enough to justify the expense).

The pen is mightier than the sword. But is it tough enough to stand up to daily use? It depends, of course, on the kind of writing you do. If to you writing means signing credit card receipts, then a fountain pen probably isn't your ticket, since it's difficult to press hard enough to make a decent impression on all the layers. However, if you see yourself composing love notes or scripting thank-you notes using your finest penmanship, then you may demand the romance and style of a fountain pen.

On the ball. Ballpoint and roller-ball pens are less work—no need to refill the ink reservoir and less risk of smears—but they don't give you much range of line width. The difference between these two types of pen is the ink they use: Ballpoints use oil-based ink and roller-balls use water-based ink.

That's Bull

Fountain pen manufacturers make quite a fuss about the purity of the gold in the nib. Expensive pens have 14k gold nibs, and even more expensive pens have 18k gold, some with platinum insets. Cheap pens employ stainless-steel nibs, and those with snob appeal electroplate a thin layer of gold over the stainless. It's not the metal in the nib that matters, it's the shape. Nibs come in different widths and shapes, depending on writing style. Scribble a bit with several different pens before settling on the one that's write—or right—for you.

Scribble, doodle, draw, and dot. Whether a fountain pen, ballpoint, or roller-ball, you should put a pen through its paces before settling on which one to buy. After all, choosing a pen is a matter of personal preference, depending on how it glides across the paper, how it feels in your hand, how it looks on the page. A good pen can make writing a pleasure; unfortunately, however, it can't help you overcome writer's block.

■ BRIGHT IDEAS: BUYING THE BEST LIGHTBULBS FOR THE MONEY

Even if you'd rather turn on a single light than curse the darkness, you may be in the dark about what kind of lightbulb to use. It was easy back in the days when the choice consisted of which wattage incandescent bulb to use. Nowadays, in addition to choosing the correct wattage, you must also weigh the pros and cons of using compact fluorescent and halogen bulbs.

They all turn on with the flip of a switch. But they work differently:

- _Incandescent bulbs_ use electricity to heat a tungsten filament that glows with slightly yellow light. It's a tried-and-true method of shedding light on the situation, but it's not too efficient. Incandescent bulbs provide more heat than light; less than 5 percent of the electrical energy used to power the bulb goes to producing visible light. Most of the energy goes to making those little glass spheres so hot your fingers fry if you grab one that's been burning for a while.

- _Fluorescent bulbs_ allow electricity to pass through a gas-filled tube. The electrons and gas atoms collide, producing ultraviolet radiation and causing a phosphor coating on the inside of the bulb to glow.

- *Halogen bulbs* work like incandescent bulbs in that they use a tungsten filament to create light; however, the halogens are filled with halogen gas, which prolongs the filament's life.

Shedding some light on the matter. Most people assume that the wattage measures how much light comes out of a lightbulb, but that's not always true. The amount of light emitted is measured in lumens, and both fluorescent and halogen bulbs produce more lumens per watt than regular incandescent bulbs. Ironically, these brighter bulbs are also more energy efficient: Fluorescent bulbs are two to four times more efficient, and halogen bulbs about one-third more efficient than the plain old incandescent variety when comparing the amount of light produced per watt of power used.

Don't Forget to Ask

Utility companies want their customers to use compact fluorescent bulbs. More fluorescents mean lower energy demands, which means postponing construction of new plants, which means fewer environmental battles with customers and less expense. The upshot of this high-energy drama: Plenty of utility companies are subsidizing the cost of fluorescent bulbs to their customers. Before shelling out top dollar for the bulbs at a hardware store or lighting specialty shop, call your utility company and ask if they offer a special deal on these efficient bulbs.

The more you spend, the more you'll save. This isn't usually true, but it may be when it comes to lightbulbs. Lots of people shy away from fluorescent compact bulbs when they look at the price tags—$15 to $30 for a single bulb, instead of about $1 or so for the regular incandescent bulbs they're used to buying. The cost-saving secret is life expectancy: Fluorescent bulbs last longer, a lot longer, than incandescent bulbs. On average, 75-watt incandescent bulbs last 750 hours (lower-wattage bulbs last about 1,000 hours); compact fluorescents can last 10,000 hours or so. That's a lot less bulb changing over the long haul.

Not so clear. Halogen bulbs may or may not save money; it depends on how much you pay for them. Compared to incandescent lightbulbs, halogen bulbs last longer, about 3,000 hours or so, and they use somewhat less energy. Longer life and lower operating costs can yield savings if you pay $4 or $5 for a halogen bulb, or they can cost more than incandescent bulbs if you pay $9 or $10 per bulb. The margin of savings is narrower, so if you want to give the halogens a try, look for them when they're on sale.

You're looking a little blue. Standard fluorescent tubes aren't well suited for home use because they cast a "cool" light that brings out blues and dulls reds. The result: a sickly, sallow complexion. Compact fluorescent bulbs don't cast the same unnatural blue that standard fluorescent tubes often do because they have a phosphor coating on the bulb that gives the same "warm" feeling as traditional incandescent bulbs. For the most true-to-daylight look, halogen bulbs beat them all; halogens cast a whiter light that's less yellow than incandescents.

Tight squeeze. Compact fluorescent bulbs screw into the socket like regular incandescent bulbs; however, they come in a variety of odd shapes and sizes that make them tough to fit in some light fixtures and under some lamp shades. Before buying, make sure that you can return the bulb if it doesn't fit in the fixture you have in mind.

■ Cleaning Your Clothes Without Being Taken to the Cleaners

Dry cleaning isn't "dry" at all. First, the operator checks the clothes over for spots and stains, treating these tough spots one at a time. Then your soiled clothes get loaded into a machine that looks a lot like a traditional washing machine, only instead of water and detergent, your clothes are cleansed with solvents. A good cleaner knows how to use the right chemical for the job; a lousy one either leaves the stains or damages the fabric—or both.

Pressing matters. After the cleaning process is complete, the cleaner presses the garment (when it comes to dry cleaning we deal with garments, not plain old clothes). Textured fabrics, such as velvets, are put on forms and steamed from the inside. Dry cleaners have a variety of pressing machines for different clothing items; these machines can usually produce a crisper finish than hand pressing. Many women's shirts are too small to fit on the man's shirt press, so they must be done by hand, which is why some dry cleaners charge more to clean a woman's shirt.

Look for a shop filled with dummies. Torso dummies, of course. Gowns and dresses should be treated on dummies; suits should be put on shoulder shapers. Other signs of a quality cleaner: Your clothes will have tissue-stuffed shoulders when they are returned to you.

Leave the faded look for your blue jeans. When cleaning a suit, bring in both pieces—the pants (or skirt) and jacket—just in case the colors fade or change slightly in the cleaning process. You won't save money in the long run if your penny-pinching at the dry cleaners means you have to replace your suit sooner.

Trivia to Impress Your Friends

Some stains don't show up until after you clean your clothes. These so-called invisible stains often occur when you spill food or beverages on your clothing, then blot it up and allow the area to dry. It looks spotless at first, but over time or with the application of heat, a brown or yellow stain appears as the sugar in the food or drink is oxidized. (The process is much like that of a peeled apple that turns brown after a few minutes in the open air.)

Don't wait for the movie. Read the care labels on your clothes. If the label says "Do not dry clean," believe it. The manufacturer isn't trying to put dry cleaners out of business; there is some reason your clothes should not be dry cleaned. For example, you shouldn't dry clean garments with rubber, nylon, or plastic parts. Likewise, take the manufacturer at his word when the label says "Dry clean only."

Blots on your record don't count. Blots on your blouses do. When you drop your clothes off, fess up: Point out any stains or discolorations so that the cleaner can take note of them. If a spot is apt to be a problem, the cleaner will have a chance to warn you that it might not come clean. Also, the operator has a better chance of getting a stain out if he or she knows what got the stain in. Also, try to eliminate new stains by removing pens and other items stuffed in your pockets before having your clothes cleaned.

It's not just the tiger who lost its stripes. During the 1980s, a number of 100 percent cotton shirts with colored stripes lost their stripes. After cleaning, the white threads were intact, but they had been stripped of their bright-colored reactive dyes. Dry cleaners and professional launderers now know how to process these shirts with a special rinse cycle to avoid damage. If your striped shirt isn't so marked, be sure to tell your cleaner to "Commercial launder in a pH-controlled scour." (The cleaner should know what this means; if not, find another cleaner.)

Don't try this at home. Leave the stains to the pros. If you try to get a stain out yourself, you're apt to make matters worse. Blot it dry and bring the garment to the cleaners ASAP.

On the mend. In addition to cleaning your clothes, many dry cleaners will make minor repairs, such as replacing buttons or stitching hems, free or for a nominal charge. If you're clumsy with a needle and thread, let your cleaner sew you up.

You want it when? Any day but today. Sure a lot of cleaners offer same-day service, but many will do a rushed and sloppy job when pressed for time. You may also pay less for second-day service.

More Trivia to Impress Your Friends

Dry cleaning can be a dirty business, but it used to be a dangerous business as well. Early dry cleaners used solvents containing camphene, benzene, kerosene, and gasoline, which were flammable and some of which were carcinogenic. In 1926, perchloroethylene, a nonflammable solvent, was introduced, and it is still used by most cleaners today.

This was a $5,000 blouse . . . really. If a dry cleaner misplaces or damages a garment, you're entitled to reimbursement, but the amount is negotiable. The cleaner wants to keep you happy—most local cleaners depend on maintaining a good reputation to stay in business—but not at any price. There are a number of factors to consider, including the original price of the garment and how much it was worth when it was brought to the cleaner. This is when your expert negotiating skills will come in handy, but don't expect to get back the full replacement cost.

Can you spot a lousy dye job? Some clothing manufacturers don't use colorfast dyes, and the color bleeds during cleaning. (This is especially problematic with dark colors and silk and rayon fibers.) In other cases, coloring on buttons or trim may transfer, rendering your favorite blouse suitable for the secondhand store. In such cases, the problem lies with the clothing manufacturer, not the cleaner. So complain, complain, complain: first to the cleaner, next to the retailer where you bought the garment, then to the manufacturer who made it. Perhaps one of them will do right by you.

■ STOP SQUINTING AND PUT YOUR SUNGLASSES ON

Sunglasses not only affect how you see, they also affect how you are seen by others. Sure, shades shield the glare of too much sun, but they also project your style, your image, your sophistication. Some people hide behind their sunglasses; others draw attention to themselves by choosing neon colors or mirrored lenses.

Too much of a good thing. The problem with excessive sunlight is that the ultraviolet light can damage the eyes, possibly causing or contributing to the formation of cataracts. If you spend an afternoon in the sun without wearing any shades, you can temporarily burn your cornea, which can make your eyes feel dry, gritty, and sore. Most of the concern involves UVB rays, which include the shortest wavelengths of light reaching the earth. Longer wavelengths of UVA rays can also cause problems, but not to the same degree.

Sunglasses at night. Some dark sunglasses can make a sunny afternoon feel like dusk, but you can't tell from the amount of tint or the degree of darkness how much of the ultraviolet light is being filtered out. Check the label to be sure. Some sunglasses, even those with only a modest tint, boost the amount of UV absorption by applying special lens coatings.

I didn't think it was so complicated. Alas, even buying a $5 pair of sunglasses for a day at the beach requires reading the fine print on the label. Sunglass manufacturers must label their wares with the degree of UV absorption: "Cosmetic" models filter out 70 percent of the UVB; "General purpose" models block 95 percent of the UVB and most of the UVA as well; and "Special Purpose" glasses (designed for sports or other activities) cut out 99 percent of the UVB rays. The U.S. Food and Drug Administration plans to require that all sunglasses screen out at least 99 percent of UVB rays and 95 percent of UVA, but the earliest the ruling could go into effect would be late 1995.

That's Bull

Some people claim that sunglasses that don't filter out all the ultraviolet rays can be harmful to your eyes, because they allow the shaded pupils to dilate, actually inviting even greater amounts of UV light into the eyes. Forget it. For one thing, even very dark glasses won't cause the pupils to dilate much. And for another, even the most basic sunglasses would screen out enough UV rays to more than make up for the minimal dilation.

True colors. Forget the fashion colors. Stick with sunglasses tinted neutral gray or gray with a hint of brown or green. These lenses distort color least. A quick test to see if the lenses are dark enough: Put on the glasses and stand two feet away from a mirror. If you can't see your eyes, the lenses are dark enough.

What you see is what you get. Not quite. Some sunglasses can actually improve your vision under certain conditions. Polarized lenses, for example, cut reflected glare, making them ideal for driving and that day on the boat or at the beach.

"How do I look?" Just take off your mirrored sunglasses and take a peek. So-called flash glasses have a very thin metallic coating that reflects most of the light. If you like the look, indulge yourself, just be aware that the coatings can be scratched easily.

Just like umbrellas. Some people leave their sunglasses at the store, at a friend's house, on the roof of the car—everywhere but across the bridge of their noses. These folks may do best to buy cheap sunglasses and use them almost like disposables: When one pair breaks or is lost, simply buy another. That can be a reasonable approach, since the UV protection can be just as good in a pair of $4 sunglasses from the drugstore as an $85 pair of Serengeti Drivers. For the extra money you're buying the frames, the style, the brand label. The choice is yours.

■ OVEREXPOSED: SELECTING THE RIGHT SUNSCREEN

All the talk about skin cancer from too much sun has changed the way society looks at a deep, dark tan—sort of. While conscious of the risk, many of us still look for bathing-suit lines after a day at the beach. If you want to enjoy the outdoors without extensive exposure to dangerous ultraviolet radiation, glob on the sunscreen.

Beyond the Bronzed Age. Face it: A tan fades but wrinkles last forever. In order to get that tan, your skin must suffer some damage. A tan is actually the body's defense against assault by the sun. About 15 percent of the white population with ultra-fair skin should reconcile themselves to their pale and freckled fate—and then wear sunscreen for maximum protection. People with light to medium complexion who can and want to tan should still wear sunscreen to avoid excessive sun as they gradually build a tan. Dark-skinned people can get by with a somewhat less protective sunscreen.

That's Bull

So-called sunless tanners don't tan the skin at all; they stain it. Granted, self-tanner sounds a lot better than self-stainer, but no self-respecting manufacturer would put out such an unappealing sounding product. Most of today's sunless tanning products contain dihydroxyacetone (DHA), a harmless pigmenting agent that produces a reddish-brown color when it binds with amino acids in the outer layers of the skin. It penetrates only the surface layers of the skin, so your tan only lasts long enough for these dead cells to slough off. Beware: Because sunless tanners only stain the skin, they don't provide any kind of "base tan," and they offer no protection against sunburn or skin cancer.

Can't get too much of a good thing. The intensity of a sunscreen is measured by its SPF, or "sun protection factor.'' The SPF is based on the amount of sunlight exposure you can tolerate before turning pink. For example, an SPF 15 sunscreen would keep you from turning pink for fifteen times as long as you would without protection. Look for a sunscreen with an SPF of at least fifteen—twenty-five or thirty is better. Technically, SPF 15 should provide enough protection, but why not build in a little extra margin for error in case you don't use enough or accidentally wipe some off.

Reach for the sun. One exception to the SPF 15 rule is when you're at high altitudes or vacationing at the equator. The intensity of the sun, and therefore the speed at which you'll suffer a sunburn, varies depending on where you're doing your basking. Tanning at the equator will cause you to burn twice as fast as you would in the northeastern United States. The closer you are to the sun, the faster you'll burn: The intensity of radiation at 5,000 feet is about 20 percent greater than it is at sea level.

Let the sun shine? All sunshine is not created equal. Ultraviolet radiation is divided into UVA (which causes wrinkles and also contributes to skin cancer) and UVB (which causes sunburn and also contributes to skin cancer). Look for a sunscreen that blocks both UVA and UVB; most say they provide ''broad-spectrum protection'' right on the label. Recent research indicates that UVA may contribute to the formation of deadly melanomas and UVB may increase risk of less deadly basal-cell and squamous-cell carcinomas.

Don't delay. Some sunscreen manufacturers simply advise you to slather on a dose before heading out to play. What they aren't telling you is that you should apply the sunscreen thirty minutes before going out so that the ingredients will have a chance to penetrate the skin. Don't want to stay inside? Then go out and nap in the shade for half an hour. You can wait.

I'm gonna wash that 'screen right out of my

hair. Waterproof sunscreens do their best to stand up to pools and ocean waves, but they won't last all day. A "waterproof" sunscreen will maintain its SPF for eighty minutes in the water; a "water-resistant" product will last only forty minutes. "Sweat-proof" brands are formulated not to run into your eyes while you're playing tennis or jogging on the beach. Keep one eye on your watch so you know when it's time to reapply.

A little dab *won't* **do you.** Most manufacturers recommend that you use one ounce to cover your body and to achieve the advertised SPF protection. That's far more than most of us apply; most people only apply half as much sunscreen as they need to. If you refuse to slather it on, you won't get the full SPF protection. For example, if you don't apply enough of an SPF 15 product, it might only provide as much protection as an SPF 8 sunscreen applied properly. A rule of thumb: Slop on a palmful of lotion and work it into your skin. There should be a thin film of unabsorbed sunscreen even after you've rubbed it in as much as possible.

Just do it . . . again. Be sure to reapply sunscreen if you towel-dry after swimming. But that second dose doesn't extend the period of protection. If you were wearing an SPF 8 that protected you for two hours, you can't apply it again and think you can stay out another two hours.

Child's play. Children can be sensitive to certain ingredients in sunscreen, particularly PABA (para-aminobenzoic acid). So-called baby sunscreens do without the irritating chemicals; if you have sensitive skin, go ahead and pamper yourself by using PABA-free products. Look for a PABA-free adult product, since "baby" brands often cost more.

Trivia to Impress Your Friends

One in seven Americans will develop skin cancer, and about 90 percent of the cancers will be linked to sun exposure. Save yourself; save your skin. Minimize your exposure, especially between the hours of 10:00 A.M. and 2:00 P.M., when the sun is strongest. Wear broad-spectrum sunscreen. Don't worship the sun; respect it.

■ DON'T TAKE IT WITHOUT LYING DOWN: BUYING BEDDING

You'll spend about a third of your life in bed (if you're getting enough sleep that is). When it comes to feeling well rested, both the quality of sleep and quantity matter a great deal. One secret to a good night's sleep is finding the right resting place.

First, some of the basics. There are three main types of mattress:

■ **Innerspring mattresses**: These consist of coiled metal springs sandwiched between layers of cushioning and covered with fabric; underneath the mattress, a box-spring foundation provides additional support. The box spring also contains coiled springs or torsion bars.

■ **Foam mattresses**: These are made of either a solid block of polyurethane foam or a foam-rubber sandwich consisting of various layers of foam of differing density that have been laminated together. A foam mattress can be placed on a wood platform or used on top of a conventional box spring.

- **Waterbed mattresses**: These are basically thick vinyl bags filled with water; mattresses range from "full-motion" to "waveless," depending on the design and amount of water. Within the universe of waterbeds, there are two main subtypes: hardside (a vinyl watermattress, liner, and heater in a rigid frame) and softside (a hybrid bed that looks like a conventional innerspring mattress but contains vinyl chambers that are filled with water).

- **Futons**: These are Japanese mattresses filled with cotton, foam, wool, or polyester. They are usually sold with a frame and function as convertible furniture, usually doubling as a sofa during the day and a bed at night. The mattress is held together by knots or tufts; the more tufts the better the mattress. Look for a futon with tufts every five to eight inches.

So many choices, so many ways to go wrong. You might be tempted to give up in despair and sleep on the floor, but don't.

Act like Goldilocks. Remember her? She's the kid who crawled into Mama Bear's bed and found it too soft, then tried out Papa Bear's bed and found it too hard. Take it from Goldilocks, finding the bed that feels *just right* depends on searching until you find one that combines the proper balance of firmness and ability to conform to your body. There is no best bed; it's up to you to find one that you'll like to spend a lot of time in. You're going to have to sleep on the job. Don't be shy: Curl up in the fetal position if that's how you sleep. And stay in bed for more than a minute or two. Any bed will feel good for sixty seconds; give yourself time to think about how it would feel for eight hours.

Are you a conformist or a nonconformist? Either way, you'll want a mattress that will support your body at all points, without bending your spine excessively. Talk with your spouse or bedmate about your preferences; in fact, the two of you should do the testing together.

Why not just sleep on the floor? That's one way to ensure firm support. If you insist on a bed, however, the semantics get tricky. Naming degrees of firmness is basically meaningless; one brand's Super Firm is another brand's Ultra Deluxe. At best, the descriptions can help compare firmness within the brand line. You're simply going to have to kick your shoes off, crawl into bed, and test it for yourself.

What you can't see can hurt you. You can't see inside your mattress, so you'll have to do your homework to find out what's going on in there. As a rule of thumb, a full-size innerspring mattress should have at least 300 coils or springs, a queen should have 375, and a king should contain at least 450. You also need to consider the wire gauge or thickness of the coils; the lower the gauge number the firmer (and better) the wire. For example, a thirteen is thicker than a sixteen. You shouldn't be able to feel the individual springs beneath the insulation and cushioning. If you can feel the springs, roll over and climb into another bed.

As for a foam bed, look for a minimum density of 2 pounds per cubic foot. In general, the higher the number, the better the foam. When shopping for a waterbed, look for one with vinyl that is at least twenty mil thick that meets the California Waterbed Standards (this is a good guideline, even if you don't live in California).

Quiet, I'm sleeping. Listen to your bed when you're rolling around. A good mattress and foundation won't crunch, creak, or wobble. Don't worry about the occasional ping, they're to be expected with an innerspring mattress.

Life on the edge. Beds with firm middles don't always have firm edges. When doing your bed tests, sit on the sides as well as the snooze position. A cheap mattress will give way at the edges, and you'll have to fight to keep from falling onto the floor.

Feel the squeeze. The average person moves forty to sixty times a night, including more than ten full body turns. To avoid feeling cramped, and ending up in divorce court, buy a bed that fits. A twin mattress is only about thirty-eight or thirty-nine inches wide, big enough for a child or an adult who doesn't flail around too much. A full-sized or double bed, which measures a mere fifty-four inches, is roomy enough for one but crowded for two. In fact, if you have two people in a double bed, each sleeper has only about as much space as a baby in a crib. A queen-sized bed provides a more generous sixty inches in width and seventy-two inches in length; it's generous for most twosomes. A king-sized mattress is the same length as the queen, but provides an extra sixteen inches of stretching room in width. Many loving couples find king-sized beds unnecessarily big; they may be designed more for people who don't want to touch—even by accident—during the night.

They won't throw you in jail, but don't remove the tag. Of course you have the legal right to deface the product labels on your mattress and pillow in the privacy of your own home after they're paid for, but don't do it. You'll need the information on the label to identify the product if you need to make a warranty claim. Find another way to express your hostility and defy authority.

Handle with care. Those little handles on the sides of larger mattresses are there for a reason: They're supposed to make it easier on you when it's time to rotate and flip your mattress. Every couple of months, shift the position. This really will equalize the wear and tear that's bound to occur.

Hide the money in the mattress, don't spend it

on the mattress. Actually, you will need to spend a fair chunk of change on a new mattress set, but that doesn't mean you should pay list price. Mattresses are often marked down to about half list price, especially around Presidents' Days sales. You can pay anywhere from $100 to $3,000; most decent ones cost about $500 or so.

■ OFF THE RACK: RECOGNIZING QUALITY CLOTHING

Whether you're shopping in a designer shop or an off-price clothing store, it pays to develop a sharp eye for quality. You don't necessarily need to spend a fortune to look good, but you do need to know what to look for. Keep these seven tips in mind:

1. Make sure the stripes and plaids are carefully matched at the seams.

2. Buttonholes should be neat and securely stitched, evenly spaced, and fit the buttons tightly. Horizontal buttonholes are more difficult (and more expensive) than vertical ones.

3. Wool collars should have felt backing to help them retain their shape.

4. Linings should not be attached all around.

5. Seams and hems should be finished and the edges should be treated so they won't fray.

6. Machine hems should be sewn with a fine blind-stitch thread. On the outside there should be a small smooth "bite." Except for very full skirts, there should be at least a two-inch hem as a sign of quality. Invisible nylon thread can be irritating because the hems don't stay in as well, and they can be scratchy.

7. Any gathers should be even; the fabric shouldn't be a series of tiny pleats.

■ THE FIR'S NOEL: CHOOSING THE RIGHT TREE FOR THE SEASON

When it comes to choosing a live Christmas tree, you don't need a degree in horticulture to find a serviceable one. That's not to say the decision should be taken lightly. The more you know about making your way through the Christmas tree lot, the more likely you will find the right tree at the right price.

First, a few basics. Most Christmas trees are either pines, firs, or spruces. Each type has its own characteristics. For example, firs tend to have a nice strong fragrance; Scotch pines and Fraser firs hold out nice firm branches that are strong enough to support weighty decorations. If you have a tree-climbing cat, consider a blue spruce; these trees have stiff needles that are sharp enough to discourage even the spunkiest household cat from going out on a limb.

Whether you buy a tree off a lot or from a cut-it-yourself tree farm, expect to pay by the foot. Most trees go for about $3 to $5 a foot, with firs at the more expensive end of the spectrum and pines at the cheaper end.

Getting fresh. You want a fresh tree, one that has been recently cut. Put your prospective tree through a freshness test: Bend the needles back; they should feel springy and resilient, not dry and brittle. You might also lift the tree a few inches off the ground and drop it. If the needles cascade to the floor, the tree may be too dry.

Don't shed on me. Some trees hold fast to their needles; others drop them at the first sign of Christmas lights. In general, Scotch pines and Douglas firs, two of the most popular types of tree, retain their needles well. Spruce trees, on the other hand, shed like a Persian cat in mid-July. Christmas trees are like giant fresh flowers; they're alive when first cut and continue drinking and breathing for several weeks longer—if they are properly cared for.

That's Bull

No need to concoct exotic Christmas tree beverages of water and aspirin and Karo syrup. Simple tap water will quench any tree's thirst, without leaving a sticky film in the bottom of your tree base at the end of the season. If the water tends to get slimy, you can add about a tablespoon of bleach. This will kill the nasty bacteria that produce the slippery gook around the base of the tree.

If you thought fresh flowers drink a lot... Then just wait until you see your Christmas tree suck down a gallon of water the first twenty-four hours you have it home. Expect it to guzzle several quarts a day after that. Make it easy on the tree to drink: Choose a tree with a moist, sticky stump, then cut off about a half inch or so at the base before putting it in water. When a tree is cut and exposed to air, sap seals the base to keep moisture in the tree. You need to make a fresh cut to break the seal and allow the tree to take in the water.

Only the hairdresser knows for sure. Most people have no idea that many Christmas trees wear a thin layer of green spray paint. Yes, it's true. According to the National Christmas Tree Association, some live trees aren't green enough to meet public approval. After they are cut, some trees go into a dormant stage and turn sort of yellow, so a light misting of green latex paint leaves the trees with that fresh-from-the-forest green tint. So natural, in fact, that you'll probably have to look closely to find out whether your tree has had its needles colored. (Expect to see brown roots either way.)

No need to needle you about cleanup. On the way into the house, most fresh trees stay in one piece. But after the holidays and several weeks in the living room, any tree begins falling apart. Consider slipping the tree into a Christmas tree body bag before dragging it outside. You may be able to contain the mess so that you will only need to sweep the area where the tree was standing. If you choose to drag a six-foot dead tree through your house, you can expect to be finding needles under the couch and behind the curtains until well after the Fourth of July.

Trivia to Impress Your Friends

Believe it or not, Christmas trees are good for the environment. For every live Christmas tree harvested, two or three seedlings are planted. Every one of these trees absorbs carbon dioxide and releases oxygen. In fact, each acre of trees planted provides the daily oxygen requirements of 18 people. Don't worry about all those end-of-the-season tree carcasses. They are biodegradable and can be turned to compost; artificial plastic trees, on the other hand, will eventually wind up in landfills where they will take about 500 years to break down. You can breathe easy when you buy a live tree.

Uncle Sam moonlights in the pest-control business. During the holidays you should have visions of sugar plums dancing in your head, not fears of pine shoot beetles hitchhiking into your home on the back of your Christmas tree. In the wild, all sorts of nasty bugs and insects nest in Christmas trees, but these little creatures are evicted before the trees make their way to market. The U.S. Department of Agriculture monitors harvested products, including crops of Christmas trees, and sets standards that ensure that your home won't be infested by anyone but your relatives over the holidays. (If you plan to cut it yourself, ask if the trees are bug-free before you bring one home.)

■ HOW MUCH IS THAT DOGGIE IN THE WINDOW?

When you return home after a vicious day in the dog-eat-dog world, your best friend is there to greet you—and maybe to lick your face. Dogs are more than mere pets; they are trustworthy, loyal, and kind companions. Treat your dog right and you can nourish a relationship far stronger and more reliable than you can with many people (sad, perhaps, but true).

Getting a dog should not be an impulse decision. If you're a dutiful dog-owner, you're entering a relationship that may last fifteen years or longer. That adorable puppy in the window needs to be walked every few hours, and it deserves your constant attention and training. To find the right dog, you need to know what to expect from the dog —and what the dog has a right to expect from you.

Ain't nothin' but a hound dog. Your first consideration should be the type of dog you think you want. Size alone is not enough to go on. You'll have to consider what characteristics the dog was bred to enhance. Each of the 135 breeds of dog recognized by the American Kennel Club has been bred to accentuate certain traits.

Of course, you can't generalize by breed. Socialization and how the dog is treated in its early life can have a huge impact on its personality, but the breed does indicate some genetic predisposition toward certain qualities.

- *Sporting dogs* (spaniels, setters, pointers, retrievers) were bred to locate game and retrieve it; with the exception of Labradors and Newfoundlands, they aren't particularly protective or good with children.

- *Hound dogs* Part 1 (beagles, bassets, dachshunds, bloodhounds) locate prey by scent. *Hound dogs* Part 2 (Afghan, Irish wolfhound, Scottish deerhound) locate prey by sight and run it down with their speed. Scent hounds may be able to tolerate life indoors; sight hounds need plenty of room to run.

- *Herding dogs* (shepherds, malamutes, huskies, collies, sheepdogs) are among the most intelligent and protective breeds. They're used to hard work, but they can tolerate indoor living as long as they get regular exercise.

- *Working dogs* (Akita, Doberman pinscher, boxer, St. Bernard) are bred to pull carts and to search and rescue. They tend to be large and strong, and they need regular exercise.

- *Terriers* (Airedale, Scottish, Welsh, fox, miniature schnauzer) are generally the most alert and active dogs. They're bred to kill rats and dig fox and otter from their dens. They're protective, energetic, and tend to be good with children.

- *Toy dogs* (Pekinese, toy poodle, Chihuahua, Maltese, Pomeranian) were bred to be the playthings of royalty and nobility. Because they can be tiny and fragile, they aren't good in homes with small children.

- *Nonsporting dogs* (chow-chow, dalmatian, poodle,

bulldog) are basically dogs that don't fit nicely into the other categories.

You need your space. And your dog needs space, too. But don't automatically assume that a small dog is best for an apartment. Some small dogs are active and need lots of space, while some larger dogs are content to lie down and rest all day. Talk to other dog owners before settling on a breed if you live in an apartment.

Finding a dog at the library. Before heading off to the pound, the pet store, or the breeder, go to the library and check out a couple of books about dogs. You probably aren't aware of all the choices out there; you may not know a shih tzu from a Lhasa apso. And even if you end up going to the pound to pick out a homeless pup, you'll have a better understanding of what personality traits and behaviors you can expect from certain breeds.

Trivia to Impress Your Friends

All dogs will bark when someone enters their turf, right? Nope. The basenji cannot bark. Physically unable to bark, these dogs make unusual chortling and yodeling sounds when happy.

Pound hound or pedigree pooch? That is the question, and there is no right answer. Your dog's fate is sealed by genetics, environment, and a roll of the dice. A purebred gives you some predictability of character due to selective breeding. Mixed breeds have mixed gene pools—you won't know what you're going to get until the puppy is grown. At a top-quality breeder, you can get a pedigree dog with some confidence that the dog will look and act like you expect it to. However, with poorly bred dogs and those from pet stores supplied by so-called puppy mills, you can't be sure what traits are swimming around in a dog's gene pool even if the dog looks like a pure-breed pup.

Money can't buy you love. Unless you use it to buy a dog. You can get a puppy free from a friend's litter, for about $25 from an animal shelter, or for $250 to $500 from a breeder. Of course, you can pay more, but you shouldn't have to unless you're after a special dog for breeding, in which case you're talking about a hobby or business, not a family pet. Some shelters also charge more, about $75 or so, because they include a fee for spaying or neutering.

Key Lingo

A dog's accomplishments at dog shows are listed on its official pedigree. Among the various codes used in dog registration papers, you'll find:

CH (Champion): *The dog has won an AKC bench championship.*

FCH (Field Champion): *The dog has demonstrated its ability to locate hiding birds, retrieve fallen birds, or track and chase game.*

CD (Companion Dog): *The dog obeys basic commands on and off the leash.*

CDX (Companion Dog Excellent): *The dog also retrieves and jumps hurdles.*

UD (Utility Dog): *The dog obeys hand signals and locates objects by scent.*

TD (Tracking Dog): *The dog can follow human scent.*

OTCh (Obedience Trail Championship): *The dog has won high awards in many obedience competitions.*

PsyW (Psychic Wonder): *The dog can actually anticipate your commands and communicate telepathically. (Just kidding.)*

This dog could have arrived on the Mayflower.
Certain blue-blood dogs have pedigrees that put them at the
top of the canine social register. If you buy a purebred dog,
be sure you receive the American Kennel Club registration
certificate. This is little more than a memento for your
scrapbook, unless at some point you want to breed the dog.

Vive la difference. Male or female? Chances are
you already have a preference. In general, males fight, wander, chase cars, demand independence, and express aggres-
sion more than females. Females are more protective,
gentler, easier to teach. One most basic difference: Males
lift their legs, so if you have expensive shrubbery outdoors
or an expensive couch indoors, keep this in mind.

A puppy is more than a small dog. Don't be
fooled: That adorable little tail-wagging fluff ball can also be
a powerhouse and a terror. Ideally, you should adopt a pup
when it's between six and twelve weeks old. Expect to
spend an enormous amount of time during the first year
working on training and nurturing. If you don't have the
time or energy to do this, consider an older dog. They're
often calmer, larger, and already trained. (Your carpets will
thank you.)

I'd like you to meet my mom and dad. Before
you settle on the dog you think you want, do your best to
meet the rest of the dog's family. You can learn a lot about
a dog by looking over his parents. Are they healthy? Well
mannered? Nervous?

Introductions all around. Not only do you want
to see your dog's parents, you want to make sure that
everyone in your family has a chance to meet with the new
dog. You want to be sure the dog gets along with everyone
—and that everyone gets along with the dog *before* you
adopt.

Welcome home. Bring your puppy or dog home as
early in the day as possible. The earlier you settle in, the

more time the dog has to adjust to the new home before nightfall.

Believe in love at first sight. In general, the most outgoing puppy in the litter is your best bet. But don't overlook the more mild-mannered dog who is a little timid at the start. He may just be waiting a few minutes to check you out. Visit long enough for everyone to relax and get to know one another. If that pathetic little high-strung yapper in the corner continues yelping the entire time you're there, forget him. This dog is apt to stay nervous and have behavior problems throughout his life. (Isn't your life complicated enough without adding another neurotic member to your household?)

Even the most priceless pet comes with a price tag. Adopting a dog is a pricey proposition. Vet bills start piling up right away, beginning with the first visit to the vet a few days after bringing the dog home with you. Expect to spend at least $50 to $100 per year for the basic checkup, vaccinations, heartworm pills, and flea powder. And that doesn't include food.

Don't Forget to Ask

- [ ] *How big will this dog get?*
- [ ] *How does this breed get along with children?*
- [ ] *Can I see the mother? The father?*
- [ ] *What shots has this dog had?*
- [ ] *Is the dog healthy? (Check for yourself: Look for signs of a dull coat, runny eyes, listless behavior, distended tummy.)*
- [ ] *Will the dog require any special grooming? How often?*
- [ ] *Will the dog shed? How much?*
- [ ] *Will it be a good guard dog?*

Chapter Eight

GADGETS, GIZMOS, AND OTHER MONEY TRAPS

■ TIMING IS EVERYTHING WHEN BUYING ELECTRONICS

You don't want to get suckered into buying some new electronic gadget that will be outdated by the time you pay your credit card bill, but you probably don't want to be the last one on your block to join the electronic age either. So just when should you buy the latest, greatest electronic gizmo?

Wait for a grandchild. As a general rule, don't buy until the third generation of a product has been introduced. Most electronic goods are introduced, improved, or updated twice a year, so you'll have to wait about one and a half to two years after a new gadget or a clever new product feature first hits the market.

Let other people make the mistakes for you. In the early part of the life cycle of an electronic product, the manufacturers are working out the design glitches. In general, after removing the kinks, the product shrinks. Full-sized players go compact; compact players get further miniaturized. Often these newly downsized products exhibit new problems. This makes sense: There is a legitimate learning curve as the manufacturers figure out how light and inexpensive they can make certain parts without having them fall apart. Give them time. The manufacturers will get it right sooner or later (or the product won't last and you'll be glad you didn't buy one).

Good things come to those who wait. In later generations, electronic goods not only tend to break down less often, they're also equipped with more useful features, and they're cheaper. By the second year, most electronic goods have matured to the point that prices begin to drop, and by the third year they're usually as low as they're going to go. No, you won't be the person with the hot gadget that everyone else wants to play with, but in the end, your gadget will be better and cheaper than the one owned by your impatient, trend-setting neighbor.

■ CHARGED UP: BUYING BATTERIES

They're in our flashlights, our kids' toys, our cameras, even the remote control for the television. Face it, most of us live a battery-operated existence.

Batteries hang on racks next to the checkout counter because they are impulse items—''Oh yeah, I almost forgot: I should pick up a pack of AAs.'' But should you reach for the classic zinc chloride heavy-duty cells or the more expensive alkalines? Or, for that matter, should you go all the way and shell out $30 to buy a set of rechargeables and a battery charger?

It keeps going and going . . . When it comes to disposable batteries, go with alkalines. They cost more, but they run longer so they turn out to be a better value. No advanced math required. The alkalines are a better deal.

Rising from the dead. Rechargeable nickel-cadmium batteries provide a big boost of power for a couple of hours, then they die and need to be resurrected. A couple of hours in the charger and these babies are ready for business, and the best part is that they can be put through hundreds of charges. In the long run, rechargeables are the best bargain, but they are more trouble.

Sprinters and marathoners. If batteries were athletes, alkalines would be marathon runners and rechargeables would be sprinters. Alkalines put out a relatively steady amount of energy for a long time, then they gradually grow tired, giving you plenty of warning that they need to be replaced. Rechargeables, on the other hand, start out sprinting, then lose stamina and quit. This isn't a problem if you keep a spare set in the charger ready to go so that you can swap one set for another, but it can be a bother if you don't have a second set of batteries handy.

"No fair! He's not helping." It makes no sense to pair a fresh battery with a weak one. A set of batteries can produce only as much power as the weakest battery will allow. In addition to a disappointing performance, the fully charged battery could stress the weaker one, possibly causing it to leak. Always replace all the batteries for a given appliance at the same time.

That's Bull

What you see isn't always what you get. Some rechargeable D-cell batteries are really nothing more than C-size cells inside D-size shells. These frauds tend to be lighter and less expensive than a true D-cell battery. So watch out.

■ PICTURE PERFECT: BUYING A CAMERA

Taking good pictures is easier than ever. There are plenty of idiot-proof, fully-automated 35mm cameras out there, many at reasonable prices. With these cameras, you can't blame the equipment if you accidentally cut Uncle Jonathan out of the picture at the family reunion, but you can rest assured that the photograph of the rest of the group was sharply focused and properly exposed.

When shopping for a 35mm camera, you have a number of choices:

- Choose a $6 to $15 _disposable camera_ from a panoramic, underwater, telephoto, flash, or basic model. They take surprisingly good photos, especially in situations where you don't want to fuss with carrying your "real" camera.
- Some $50 to $450 _compact cameras_ have automatic focus; others have a fixed focus. These cameras have a wide range of options and settings, including built-in telephoto and zoom lenses.
- The $200 to $650 _single-lens reflex camera_ with do-it-yourself focus often comes with interchangeable lenses; some have automatic exposure control to lend you a hand in getting the right exposure.
- A $350 to $1,300 _fully-automatic single-lens reflex camera_ allows you to just show up and push the button. The camera does the rest.

More on the compacts. The compact category makes up a huge portion of the camera market, as much as 95 percent by some accounts. The range of prices for these cameras is significant. So what do you get for the money?

- Cameras in the _$75 and under category_ typically have plastic lenses and fixed focus. They claim to automatically adjust for all film speeds, but in reality most only recognize 100- and 400-speed film. (If the camera is set for the wrong speed film, the photographs will either be underexposed or overexposed, leading to washed-out colors and grainy pictures.)
- Cameras in the _$75 to $250 category_ typically have

glass lenses and zone focusing. The camera divides the image in the viewfinder into zones like those on a football field. The camera sends out an infrared beam in search of the subject; by measuring how long it takes the beam to reach the subject, the camera can calculate which zone the subject is in and set the focus accordingly. Cameras at the upper end of the price range send out multiple beams—two to five—so they stand a better chance of getting the subject in focus. These cameras usually recognize 100-, 400-, and 1,000-speed film.

- Cameras in the *$250 and higher category* have continuous focus; they contain a charge-couple device that allows the camera to actually focus on the image. These cameras recognize 100-, 400-, 1,000-, and 1,600-speed film.

Many people love their point-and-shoot cameras, because they can get good clear 35mm prints without fussing around with too many gadgets and controls. If you want good pictures and you'd rather let the camera do the work for you, buy a compact 35mm model.

What beautiful red eyes. A number of cameras now come with red-eye reduction devices built into the camera's flash. Many of these devices strobe a bright light several times before the final flash so that the subjects' eyes will dilate and red eye can be avoided. With other designs, a halogen flash precedes the shutter release to achieve the same effect. Avoid the strobe flash around people with epilepsy; the pulsating light can trigger seizures in some people.

Whose list is it? Never pay the manufacturer's list price for a camera. Discounts are *always* available, if you're willing to shop. Browse through camera magazines or the Sunday edition of the *New York Times* for mail-order discounters. Before ordering by mail, be sure you know exactly what you're ordering. Some super-low prices are for cameras with off-brand lenses or stripped down cameras and don't include other equipment that usually comes with the camera. Compare exactly what you're going to get with each deal.

It's not always black or white. Check out the "gray market." Equipment that has been imported through authorized channels comes with—and usually brags about—its U.S. warranty. Photo supplies that are imported by distributors, who aren't authorized by the factory but can legally sell the same equipment, has an "international warranty." What does this mean to you? It means you may have to send the camera back to Japan for service. Some stores sell U.S. warranties for an additional fee. Find out what kind of warranty you have before you buy.

What's that green stuff in the back of your refrigerator? Could it be film? No kidding. Unprocessed film that's been sitting around can develop mold, so keep your film sealed until you're ready to use it.

Breaking a sweat is good for you. But not for your camera. If you use your camera outdoors in cold weather, put it in a plastic bag when you come inside. The condensation that will form when the camera hits the warm air indoors will form on the bag, not the camera lens and viewfinder.

Sticky situations exist in every family. But they don't have to be in every family album. Avoid using transparent album pages made with sheets of polyvinyl chloride. Over time, the album pages made with this plastic can stick to the photographs, ruining both the album and your prints. Check with a photo supply or stationery store for appropriate albums.

■ BUYING TIME: SELECTING A WATCH

When time is of the essence, you don't need to spend a lot of money. A $20 Casio watch keeps time just as well as a top-of-the-line Rolex. In fact, a cheapo quartz watch actually keeps time better than a $15,000 14k-gold Rolex that you have to wind yourself. Even the least expensive quartz-crystal watches lose or gain only about one second a week. (Atomic clocks, on the other hand, lose no more than a second in one million years.)

There are several different types of watch mechanisms:

- *Mechanical watches* are the old-fashioned wind-up models that work by turning the mainspring.
- *Automatic* or *self-winding watches* rely on the owner to move around, causing a weight behind the movement to rotate, winding the mainspring.
- *Quartz movement watches* contain quartz crystals that vibrate more than 32,000 times per second. The watch battery sends electronic impulses through the vibrations and translates them into a fixed number of impulses per second. No more winding a mainspring to make the tiny gears whirl and twirl.

Take it at face value. When you're buying a watch, you're basically buying the extras—the design, the case, the band. If you choose a gold watch, you can either buy a pricey karat-gold case and band, which doubles as a piece of dress jewelry, or a gold-plated timepiece. The more expensive the watch, the thicker the gold plating; stick to plating at least ten microns thick, less will wear off more quickly.

Let me make this crystal clear. Watch crystals consist of mineral glass on lower-priced models, or sapphire crystals (actually a shatterproof, scratch-resistant synthetic) on watches costing $300 and up. If your crystal cracks, replace it right away. Otherwise, moisture will leak into the inner workings.

Watch out. When it comes to water, be sure your watch can take it before you go dancing in the rain. The Federal Trade Commission won't allow manufacturers to use the term "waterproof," so watches are now assessed as water-resistant to different degrees. If a watch says nothing about water resistance on the case, then assume it has no protection. (This is most common with fancy dress watches.) These watches aren't apt to grind to a halt if you wash your hands or get caught in a spring shower, but they could be in trouble if you take a dip in the pool. A watch labeled water-resistant to fifty meters can withstand showering or swimming in shallow water; one marked water-resistant to a hundred meters can be worn during swimming or snorkeling. Diving watches are specialty lines that can, of course, withstand the pressure of the ocean's depths.

Dick Tracy was almost right. Radio transmitters aren't common on wristwatches yet, but stopwatches, lunar-phase indicators, alarms, tachometers, and calculators are commonplace. Special features add to the high-tech look, but do you really want a watch that's smarter than you are? Buy only those features you'll use.

Takes a licking . . . But to keep it ticking you'll have to replace the battery every one to five years. The more gadgets to support, the faster the battery will grow weary.

■ A STAR IS BORN: DISCOVERING THE RIGHT VIDEO CAMERA

Armed with a video camera and a blank tape, you may be ready for "America's Funniest Home Videos," even if your family isn't. Alas, the price of becoming a "movie star" is lower than ever. The typical video camera or "camcorder" is about $800, with some going for as little as $500.

What are you hungry for? It depends on the machine. Full-sized VHS recorders accept the same size VHS tapes you use to record television programs on your VCR. VHS-C models accept smaller tapes that can be adapted to play like full-size VHS tapes. The 8mm models use small tapes that look like audio cassettes. There are also so-called high-band versions known as either Hi-8 or S-VHS-C, which require special tapes that produce sharper pictures at a higher price. (The high-band recorders also cost about $100 more than their basic models.)

How long is the party? If you want to capture the action from the first arrival to the time your kid blows out the birthday candles, you may prefer the 8mm models. These machines use cassettes that can record for two hours; the VHS-C cassettes hold only thirty minutes of action, unless you use the extended-play mode, in which case you can squeeze out ninety minutes, but the picture quality won't be quite as good. The downside to the 8mm is that you'll have to connect the camcorder to your VCR or TV for playback instead of popping the tape into an adapter and playing it in your VCR like you can with the VHS-C models. It's a trade-off between time and convenience. (Isn't it always?)

Such beautiful features. Generally speaking, the more you spend, the more special features and add-ons you get. Want a color viewfinder? Electronic image stabilization (to minimize the jerkiness of your movements)? A time-lapse button to record a one-second burst every minute (so that you really *can* watch grass grow)? All of these features, and more, are available if you're willing to pay for them.

When the wind blows . . . It makes noise on the tape. Video recorders have built-in microphones that capture voices just fine but don't do well with music, and make a thundering racket when the wind is blowing. If you plan to record outside or if you want to improve the music or spoken sound track, then buy a camcorder equipped with a jack for an external microphone.

Spending money to save money. When buying blank videotapes, it pays to buy the good brands. The oxide coating on the no-name or bargain brands is more likely to flake off and foul up your machine's internal workings. If you're just playing around with the machine, use standard tapes, but if you're recording something for the family archives, don't cut corners. Buy high-grade tape that will last longer. Your daughter's first birthday and high school graduation are once-in-a-lifetime experiences.

Did you see her face? When playing back a videotape, don't hold the tape in pause or still frame for an extended period. The video head moves back and forth, and it can wear down that section of the tape.

Running hot and cold. If you use your camera to shoot the family on the ski slopes while on vacation, don't rush inside and expect to play it back right away or moisture may get trapped inside the tape due to the abrupt change in temperature. Instead, allow at least half an hour before playing.

Chapter Nine

CRASH COURSE IN CAR COSTS

■ SHOWROOM SHOWDOWN: BUYING A CAR

In recent years, some new car dealers have taken much of
the sting out of haggling for a car. New straightforward
set-price shopping makes dealing with the dealer a take-it-
or-leave-it proposition that puts the buyer and dealer on a
much more even footing. Even under the old-style negotiation, you can buy a new car without being taken for a ride, as
long as you develop a car-shopping strategy and stick to it.

I can see you behind the wheel of a . . . No,
you want to buy the car that you want, not the car that the
salesperson wants to sell you. Talk to friends, read magazines, and browse the showrooms. Ask for brochures, and
review them at home before you start your serious shopping.

Shop until you drop. But once you're tired, go
home and rest. Buyers with that make-me-an-offer-I-won't-
refuse look are asking for trouble. If you're sick of looking,
take a break or else you may hate yourself in the morning.

This baby's all mine. After thirty-six monthly payments that is. Try to finance a car over two or three years;
if you need to stretch the payments out longer, you probably
can't afford that car in the first place—and you'll pay a
fortune in interest.

Out with the old, in with the new. If you can
afford to wait, shop for a new car at the end of the model
year. Car dealers need to clear out their inventories to make

That's Bull

_Walking can be very good for you—especially when a car dealer
is trying to take advantage of you. One tactic: You sign a
contract, drive the car home, then get a call from the dealer
saying that you need to pay another $900 or some such
amount because either the bank won't lend you the full
amount or there's some unforeseen problem with your trade-in._
_Forget it. In states where this practice is illegal, dealers must
either honor the contract, renegotiate from scratch, or cancel
the deal and return your money and car. Don't hand over one
red cent more; assuming the salesperson's plea for more money
is true, the fact that the dealer made a lousy business deal is
no reason for you to pay more._

room on the lot for the new cars, and many manufacturers
provide additional dealer discounts to sell those cars fast,
fast, fast.

Manipulation is a two-way street. Assume that
most car dealers will manipulate you every chance they get,
so don't feel bad about taking advantage of your situation
when you can. Shop for a car at the end of the month
when the dealer is feeling pressed to meet monthly quotas.
Negotiate until you think you've got a good deal, then say
you want to wait a couple of days—until the beginning of
the next month. You may find the dealer is suddenly able to
squeeze an even better deal out of the "manager."

Sorry, I'm not going to pay. Some dealers offer a
decent price for the car, then tell you that the car comes
with certain extras, such as undercoating, racing stripes,
fabric protectors, and other options for which you must pay
extra. Politely refuse these overpriced add-ons. If the dealer
says they've already been added, smile and refuse to pay for

them. Don't fall for this cheap ploy to nickel and dime you while trying to make you feel as if you're getting a bargain because the "real price" for these options is twice what you're asked to pay.

Trivia to Impress Your Friends

The trend toward set-price selling doesn't always mean savings for new car buyers. According to Consumer Reports *magazine, General Motors' Saturns sell at 13 percent over dealer cost, compared with the industry average of 6.7 percent for other car models.*

"I have faith that this will be a good car." Don't buy the extended service contract that covers repairs beyond the manufacturer's warranty. The dealer will make it sound like a great deal, but chances are you will pay more for the contract than you ever would for the repairs. Be suspicious whenever a salesperson is overeager to sell you something; clearly it's in his best interest, not yours.

I've got to call my broker. That's car broker, not stockbroker. Auto brokers buy cars at rock-bottom prices, then charge you a premium over the dealer cost. Brokers won't provide buying advice; you need to know what you want and the broker handles the transaction. (Before buying an imported car, make sure it meets U.S. emissions standards.) If you enjoy the game of car shopping, then you might be able to get the car from a dealer for a lower price than you could with a broker after paying the broker's commission, which is usually several hundred dollars. But using an auto broker allows you to buy the car you want at the price you want; you're basically paying for the broker to do the haggling for you.

Take this baby out for a test drive. Then take it home and park it in the driveway. Sometimes you can get a good deal by buying a low-mileage demonstration car, as long as it comes with a new-car guarantee. Even if you don't want to buy a demo, take a test drive in one anyway; you should test drive any car before you buy it.

Accidents happen. That's why you need insurance. You can pay less—sometimes significantly less—by choosing a car with special safety features, such as air bags and antilock breaks. You'll be safer, and your insurance payments may be lower, too.

"This is the extra-profit-for-me fee." The sticker might as well say that. Some stickers include a line marked ADP (Additional Dealer Profit), ADM (Additional Dealer Markup), or AMV (Additional Market Value). This is outright profiteering on sought-after models. If you don't understand a fee, ask what it means. Any add-on costs or procurement fees are negotiable; you don't have to put up with them.

Step one, buy; step two, sell. Buying a new car and selling your old one are two separate transactions. The dealer will try to mingle the two, perhaps by undervaluing the trade-in so that you can get a great "deal" on the new car. Negotiate the best deal you can on your new car, then talk trade-in.

More Bull

Some unscrupulous car dealers will strip a car of its carpeting and then try to sell it back to you for an extra fee. Before paying for any add-ons, read the brochure carefully. You may find that some of what you're being asked to pay for comes standard with the car.

■ A New Lease on Life— or at Least on a New Car

Advertisements for auto leases scream about low monthly payments, and whisper in the fine print about the details of the deal. Looking only at the bottom line, the cheapest way to get behind the wheel of a car is to pay cash or make the biggest down payment you can afford, then nurse the car into a ripe old age.

Leasing makes sense, however, for people who want a new car but can't afford the down payment or monthly payment necessary for a new car. Before considering a lease, determine approximately how many miles you expect to drive during the lease. Most companies allow you to drive about 15,000 miles a year, then you pay as much as 25 cents for each additional mile.

It's critical that you look before you leap—or lease. Following is a list of things to watch out for before signing any deal:

- Most offers hook you with the low monthly payments, failing to mention the often significant *mandatory down payment* (or "capital-cost reduction"). Find out all the details before committing yourself.
- The lease contract rarely defines what *"Excess wear and tear" charges* mean, so dealers use these fees to force drivers into another contract at the end of the lease. A driver might turn in a car and be told to pay $2,500 in end-of-lease wear-and-tear charges . . . but those charges can be dropped if you choose to lease another car. Ask that the definitions of wear and tear be clearly stated in the contract.
- Many dealers require a security deposit of several hundred dollars. Buried down in the small print of some contracts is a notice that this so-called deposit is *nonrefundable*. (Isn't that an outright fee?)

The price isn't right. Then negotiate. You can haggle just as much with a lease as you can with a car purchase. (Oh, joy.) There is a tremendous amount of flexibility in how a lease can be arranged, so shop around and see what kind of deal various salespersons can come up with.

Trivia to Impress Your Friends

Approximately one out of every five new cars on the road is leased. Among luxury models, about half are leased.

It's like handing over a blank check. Never sign an open-end lease. This type of contract leaves you financially liable if the car depreciates in value more than expected. Closed-end leases leave you with no obligation to buy the car or pay extra at the end of the lease term.

■ DRIVER FOR A DAY: RENTING A CAR

When renting a car, it's often hard to figure out how much you'll actually have to pay. You may be quoted one rate, without being told about add-ons, such as fuel charges, airport fees, additional-driver fees, mileage fees, and collision-damage waivers. These fees can double the price of the car rental and make it tough to compare prices by phone.

You can't afford not to be insured. But you might already be covered. Before handing over $7 to $15 a day for the rental company's optional collision-damage waiver to cover liability and physical damage to the car in case of an accident, check with your auto insurance company. Many policies already provide coverage for rental cars.

More is not always better. Many states require rental agencies to provide a minimal level of insurance as part of the base rental price, regardless of the extra insurance they cajole you to buy. You also want to steer clear of insurance add-ons, including those that cover you for accidents unconnected with the car.

You want to enjoy your vacation, don't you? Those thoughtful car-rental agents are always so concerned about adequate leg room and cramped luggage compartments that they urge their customers to upgrade to larger, "more comfortable" models. Don't fall for this ploy. Often the hard-sell stems from the fact that the smaller (and cheaper) models have been rented out already. Sometimes if you resist the pitch, you will still drive away in a larger car, because it may be the only car available.

Go ahead and kick the tires. Be sure you know how to turn on the headlights, the turn signals, and squirt the windshield wipers. You don't want to be merging on the expressway when you discover that you don't know where to locate all of the controls.

Hee-hee, they'll never catch me. Don't bet on it. If you get a parking ticket in a rental car, the police may go to the rental company and ask for your name. These days, many car-rental companies are complying and handing over your name, address, and license-plate number to the police. You can run, but you can't hide.

More embarrassing than getting your credit card rejected. A growing number of car-rental companies are checking their customers' driving records and refusing to rent to high-risk drivers. Some companies are pickier than others, but most reject prospective renters who have had two accidents or three moving violations within the past two years. If you have had a couple of automotive mishaps, check out the company's policy before trying to rent a car.

Running on empty. Check into whether you need

to return the car with the tank as close to full or as close to empty as possible. Some companies encourage you to come coasting in to the rental lot with an empty fuel tank—and if you leave some gas in the tank, you don't get credit for it. Others require a full tank, or else you'll pay top dollar to refill the tank. Find out before you leave the lot, so you can keep an eye on the gauge as you get ready to return the car.

Never on a Monday. Or sometimes on a Monday —it depends on the company. Most car-rental places offer weekend discounts, and different companies define "weekend" differently. Ask about any specials that might be available, including discounts associated with your airline or your employer.

Don't Forget to Ask

☐ *How much fuel will be in the car when I get it?*
☐ *How much fuel should be in the car when I return it?*
☐ *Are there any airport fees?*
☐ *Are there any additional driver fees?*
☐ *How much is the collision-damage waiver?*
☐ *Is there unlimited mileage? If not, how much will I have to pay for each additional mile over the limit?*

■ RUSTPROOFING: UNWISE AT ANY PRICE

When you buy a new car, you can be certain that the dealer is going to give you a hard sell about a number of options and service packages. With some you might have to ponder the pros and cons, but not this one: Skip the rustproofing and undercoating.

Whether done by the dealer or at an independent facility, rustproofing and undercoating isn't worth the $200 to $400 you'll be charged for it. Rustproofing involves spraying petroleum wax inside the wheel wells, panels, and other cavities of your car; undercoating consists of spraying the belly of your automobile with a tacky, tarlike substance.

"But the manufacturer says . . . " Auto manufacturers are in a tricky situation: They want to boast about how resistant their cars are to rust, but they don't want to annoy their dealers, who profit handsomely from selling additional rustproofing services to prospective car buyers. Today's cars are made of galvanized steel, which is coated with zinc and designed to resist rust. Even if parent companies shy away from condemning additional rustproofing outright, the Motor Vehicle Manufacturers Association concedes that after-market rustproofing isn't necessary.

Listen to what they *don't* tell you. Someone trying to sell you rustproofing is going to brag about the company's extended warranty against rust, perhaps for the life of your car. Interesting, huh? What they don't tell you is that the warranty covers only rust that starts on the *inside;* it doesn't include the more common rust spots that show up around scratches or chips in the exterior paint.

■ ALL WASHED UP: PICKING A CAR WASH

There are two types of people: Those who like to wash their cars, and those who don't. Often, those of us who feel self-righteous if we bathe our cars once or twice in the summer think that those who buff and wax their wheels each week are obsessive. But the truth is that the frequent washers may be on to something. In winter, you need to remove the road salt and slush; in summer, you need to remove the dusty grime and mud before it permanently damages your car's finish.

That doesn't mean you need to pull out the garden hose, draw a bucket of sudsy water, and hunt down a chamois cloth just yet. You may find it faster and easier to slip into a professional car wash. A few of your options:

■ **Self-serve:** You drive into a car wash bay, slip your quarters into the slot, and wait for the wand at the end of the hose to come to life and spray foamy water. Why the foam? "People love foam," confides a car wash expert who said the real cleaning comes from the water pressure, not the detergent. This poor man's car wash costs about $3 or $4. Keep in mind that time is money; the clock starts as soon as you put your quarter down, so read the instructions and be ready to go. With a self-service wash, your car will get as clean as you want it to—or as long as the quarters hold out.

■ **Automatic service:** Your kids will love the monster brushes and gusts of water (or else they'll be terrified and scream). With most automatic washes, someone will take about thirty seconds to zip through your car's interior with a high-suction hose, then it's off to the showers. You drive onto a conveyor, which pulls your car through a mechanical device that slathers your car with soapy water, scrubs it down, puts it through a rinse cycle, then gives it a blow dry. Your car will get reasonably clean, though tough spots and nooks and crannies may be untouched.

■ **Hand wash:** A real person will vacuum and wipe down your car's interior, then wash the outside by hand (some do a hand finish after putting the car through the automatic wash). Of course, not all full-service washes are created equal, and, as you might imagine, the more you pay the cleaner, the more showroom-new-looking your car should be. You can get a hand wash for as little as $15 or as much as $200 for a complete "detailing," which means a thorough top-to-bottom scrub down, including washing the carpets, cleaning the upholstery, and tending to every detail.

If you think my car is dirty, then you don't want to see my bathroom floor. Probably not, but the difference between the bathroom floor and your car is that the dirt on the car can actually destroy its finish. Finishes on today's cars consist of a thin layer of clear hard plastic like a top coat of nail polish. Grit and grime will stick to your car, and if you don't wash it off the gook will bake on and penetrate the finish. When the dirt eventually flakes off, it can take a layer of the finish with it, compromising the exterior of your car. In severe cases, the finish can chip right down to the metal, leaving it susceptible to rust.

That's Bull

Though the sign says "wax" the treatment sold as part of most standard car washes isn't wax at all, but a thin layer of diluted kerosene, which causes water to bead up and run off your car. This stuff is really a rinse aid that helps your car repel water. At most car washes, if you want wax you'll have to pay a couple of dollars extra for the "hot wax" treatment. You should wax your car every couple of weeks so that what is exposed to the elements is the wax, not your car's finish. The best alternative is to lovingly apply wax by hand yourself (or pay someone else to do it for you). If you don't have the time (or money) to do the job by hand, then opt for the hot wax treatment from a commercial car wash.

Alfred Hitchcock understood how dangerous birds can be. Indeed, bird droppings are among the most hazardous substances known to cars. Leave a bird dropping on your car for two or three days in the sun and you'll have a permanent mark. The combination of heat and acidity can damage any car's finish.

Don't get rubbed the wrong way. Some car washes boast that they are "brushless"; others tout that they use nonabrasive cloth strips. What difference does it really make? Virtually none. You may be shocked to learn that it's all advertising hype. Brush or brushless, sponge or cloth, all will clean your car. The friction methods do risk scratching the finish somewhat after repeated washes (you'll scratch less if you wash more frequently because your car will be less dirty), but many so-called nonfriction methods use harsh chemicals. Like everything else in life, it's a trade-off. Neither will do much harm, or they wouldn't still be in business, now would they?

Unless you have a hole in the floorboard, it's a good idea. An undercarriage spray is usually an extra for which you are charged an extra dollar or so. Since salt and dirt obviously splash up under the bottom of your car, it makes sense to spray underneath for a thorough wash.

Trivia to Impress Your Friends

☐ *Amount of water used to hand wash your car for 10 minutes in the driveway: 100 gallons.*

☐ *Amount of water used at a self-serve car wash bay: 11.1 gallons.*

☐ *Amount of water used in an automatic car wash: 55 gallons.*

Would you go a week or two without bathing?
Don't answer that. Just make sure to wash your car that
frequently. It might seem excessive at times, but it will
make your car's finish last longer. A small price to pay,
considering what you probably spent on the car.

■ SHOES FOR YOUR CAR: BUYING TIRES

Most people don't think about their tires until one goes flat.
But tires are far more technical than what meets the eye. If
you want your car to grip the road and respond to your
commands, you need to keep your tires properly inflated
and in good shape.

There are three main types of passenger tires:

- **All-season tires:** Basic tires that combine reasonable
  tread life and performance;
- **Performance tires:** Those with wider, shallower
  tread that handle well when wet but wear out more
  quickly; and
- **Touring tires**: Those that try to be super-premium
  all-season tires.

Be willing to compromise. Actually, you have no
choice. No tire can do it all. Softer rubber tires provide
excellent traction, but they wear out quickly. Stiff sidewalls
respond to steering commands, but they may not provide as
comfortable a ride.

The secret to a long life. The life expectancy of
your tires is printed right on the sidewalls, but most people
don't know how to break the code. The U.S. Department
of Transportation requires that tire manufacturers display
the tread-wear index, a measure indicating the anticipated
tread life of the tire. The tread wear of all tires is measured

against a standard reference tire graded at 100. A tread-wear rating of 360 means that the tire should last 3.6 times longer than the reference tire. Of course, actual tread wear varies with road surface, driving habits, and the type of car, but comparing the tread-wear index on several tires should give you some way of comparing relative differences in how long different tires might be expected to last.

Trivia to Impress Your Friends

If Americans kept their tires properly inflated, the United States would consume 100,000 fewer barrels of oil every day.

You wouldn't wear a high-heeled pump and a flat sandal. So don't ask your car to by mixing types of tires when buying replacements. Tires come in bias, bias-belted, and radial designs. (Almost all passenger tires are radials these days.) Stay with the same design, and keep your tires in matched sets in the front and back. Switching to a different size or type of tire can affect the ride, handling, suspension, ground clearance, and speedometer and odometer readings. Check your car's owner's manual for approved tire sizes and types.

I'm under a lot of pressure. As a tire should be. Low air pressure causes poor fuel mileage, poor handling, and excessive wear that can lead to a blowout. So why not add a little extra pressure so you won't have to refill as often? Because overinflated tires bulge and wear in the middle. Keep your tires properly inflated and they will last a lot longer.

I saw it with my own eyes. Don't trust everything you see. Radial tires can appear to be properly inflated, even when they're as low as 10 psi (pounds per square inch). You won't know unless you check.

Writing on the wall. Don't refer to your whitewall to find out how much air to put in your tires. Sure, it's a guide, but you should pull out the owner's manual and find out what your car manufacturer recommends. (The magic number may also be posted on the driver's door, the door-jamb, or in the glove-compartment.) Different cars have different demands, even on the same set of tires.

That's Bull

To protect against uneven wear, when you buy a new set of tires you should have them spin-balanced when they are mounted to the wheels. In addition to the hundreds of dollars the tires cost, some greedy dealers will try to charge an extra $3 to $6 per tire for balancing. Forget it. This simple service should be included in the price of the new tires. If the dealer squawks, take a walk.

Get 'em while they're hot. But test 'em while they're cold. Check your tire pressure when the tires have not been used, or if you use a service station gauge after driving no more than a couple of miles. The tire pressure can increase 4 to 8 psi or more when the tires become hot after driving. Ideally, you should test the pressure every forty-five days or when you significantly change the load.

Can't you tell your left from your right? Your front from your back? When it comes to tires, all four tires start out the same, then they need to be rotated to different positions on the car every 6,000 to 10,000 miles so that they wear evenly. Front and rear tires wear differently depending on driving conditions and habits and, of course, whether the car is a front- or rear-wheel drive. Belted radial tires should be moved from front to back or back to front, but they should stay on the same side of the car, since switching sides can twist the tire and cause "radial pull." Some dealers include a free rotation with the purchase of new tires, so check your tire warranty.

Listen to your tires. And look at them when they're talking to you. Tires have built-in tread indicators or wear bars that tell you when your tread is wearing thin. (They show up when the tread is worn down to one-sixteenth of an inch.) As the tread wears down these bars appear between the tread grooves; the tires need to be replaced when the bar stretches across three or more grooves. But you've got to be paying attention to notice the bars, so make a point to give your tires a quick once-over when you fill up the tank with gasoline.

Penny for your thoughts. Another way to test your tread is to stick the edge of a penny headfirst into a tread groove. If you can see the top of Lincoln's hair, it's time to replace the tires.

Don't tread on me. But do keep enough tread on the road. In addition to the wear-bar test, look for cracks or cuts in the sidewalls that are deep enough to expose the cords or interior fabric. If you can see the threads, your tires are no longer roadworthy.

Shake, rattle, and roll. Fine for the dance floor, not a great idea on the interstate. If you notice a vibration in the steering wheel that comes and goes depending on the speed you're driving, then your tires are out of balance or they are out of alignment. If you pretend like you don't notice it and continue to drive, your tires will wear unevenly, then you'll need to replace your tires, as well as get them aligned and balanced.

No one ever called. How could they when you

never filled out the registration card when you bought your tires? If you complete and return the registration card with your name, address, and tire identification code, the manufacturer can contact you in the event of a product recall.

■ TIME FOR A CHANGE: SELECTING MOTOR OIL

Without the proper amount of clean motor oil to keep the moving parts lubricated, your engine would get so hot that the metal would melt and self-destruct. No kidding. Don't let this happen to you: Be sure your car has an adequate supply of fresh motor oil.

Time for a transfusion. Oil is the lifeblood of a car; it circulates through the engine, reducing friction, cooling the engine, and helping to clean away sludge and harmful deposits. Oil works hard—hard enough that it needs to be changed regularly. The more often you change the oil, the more your car will thank you. How? With years of driving pleasure.

Chances are you aren't a normal driver. Take no offense; most of us aren't ''normal'' drivers, at least the way the auto manufacturers define normal. Their description of normal driving conditions: Driving at least twenty miles at steady highway speeds on clean, dry, paved roads. Most of us impose ''severe'' demands on our cars by taking short trips (ten miles or less), driving in stop-and-go traffic, and going out during the hot summers and cold winters. The more demanding you are of your car, the more frequently you need to change the oil. If you drive only under ideal conditions (and who does?) then you can squeak by with changing the oil every 7,500 miles. Most drivers will have

to follow a more nurturing routine and change the oil somewhere around the 3,000- or 3,500-mile mark.

Filtering out trouble. When you change the oil, go
ahead and change the oil filter, too. Some engines leave as
much as one pint to one quart of oil in the filter when the
oil is drained. If the filter isn't replaced, this contaminated
oil mixes with the fresh oil. Some automakers and mechanics
argue that the filters need only be changed every other time,
since the improved additives in today's oils help keep the
engines cleaner. The expense is minimal, but if you insist on
waiting, be sure to replace the filter with the second oil
change.

Goldilocks and the Three Oils. When picking a
motor oil, you should be as picky as Goldilocks. Start by
referring to the owner's manual for a list of acceptable types
of oil. You'll have to pick a viscosity grade (the viscosity is
the thickness of the oil at different temperatures). You don't
want the oil to be too thick (or the engine will be hard to
start) and you don't want it too thin (or the oil will be
squeezed out from between the parts); you want an oil
that's *just right.*

Change with the weather. Multigrade oils can
cover a range of different temperatures while maintaining
the correct viscosity. They perform this trick by depending
on viscosity-index improvers: the more of this additive, the
wider the range of conditions the oil can tolerate. Sounds
great, except there's a catch (of course). When they get
hot, these viscosity-index improvers break down into a car-
bonlike material that can damage the pistons. To avoid problems, stick to oils with the narrowest range available. For
example, consider a 10W-30 instead of 10W-40 oil, depending on the weather. (Your owner's manual will provide
the details.)

Behind the wheel, not under the hood. If you're
a driver who would need to spend half an hour under the

hood searching for your car's dip stick to test the oil, then go ahead and have the service station attendant add the extra quart of oil when you're low. But be aware that you're paying $2 or $3 a quart for oil that would cost half that much in retail automotive supply stores.

That's Bull

Motor oils marked "Shake well before using" may try to hype their special additives. Don't listen. If you need to shake the can before putting it in your car, then the additives aren't in suspension and have settled on the bottom of the can. Inside your car, those same additives will settle to the bottom of your engine and cause sludge build-up. Just put the can back on the shelf and look for another brand.

■ HIGHWAY ROBBERY: SHOPPING FOR AUTO REPAIRS

Almost anyone with a car can tell horror stories about getting service work or repairs done. You can avoid getting hoodwinked by following a few simple rules.

Doctor, I'd like a second opinion. Before an auto mechanic performs major surgery on your car, check the diagnosis with another shop. Be as specific as possible when describing the problem, then listen carefully to the mechanic's advice. Before agreeing to have the work done, take your car to another shop for an estimate. If you hear the same advice, it's probably accurate—and now you have two bids on the job.

The squeaky wheel really does get greased. Or the distributor cap gets replaced. Or some other repair gets done free of charge to the car owner who complains in a loud voice. Though automobile dealers are loathe to talk about it, virtually every automaker offers informal or secret warranties. When a significant number of car owners report the same problem or defect, an auto manufacturer may tell its car dealers that it will pay to cover the repair, but only for those customers who complain loudly and repeatedly. These secret warranties apply to items not covered by the regular warranty, and they are often issued to avoid a formal recall. Once again, it pays to complain.

That's Bull

How much you're going to pay for repairs will depend in large measure on how much you will have to pay in labor charges. Some shops charge a flat rate for a job. Others charge a flat hourly rate, which is then multiplied by either the actual number of hours the mechanic works under the hood or by a set rate published in a flat-rate manual. The flat-rate manual defines a specific amount of time for a certain job, say 2½ hours for a brake job. Even if the mechanic does the job in 2 hours, you'll pay the full amount. New tools and streamlined equipment allow mechanics to work faster, but you still get stuck with the old-fashioned bill.

In response to justified consumer outrage, some shops have initiated a "clock-in/clock-out" billing method. Under this novel system, a mechanic punches a time card at the beginning and end of a job, and you pay for the actual work time. Whether or not you save money depends on the hourly wage. Compare the hourly rates under both the flat-rate and clock-in methods when deciding where to get your repair work done.

Just look for someone with automotive grease under his fingernails. Finding the right repair shop is a little trickier than that. Not every shop can handle every type of repair competently. For simple repairs, go to the corner service station, but for a more complicated fix, especially one involving computerized components, stick to the dealer or a specialty shop that knows your make inside and out.

The Little Engine That Couldn't: **Volume One.** You might spend ten minutes explaining to the front office about how the engine is coughing out smoke and sputtering when you put it in neutral, only for the service representative to jot down "runs rough" on the service form. You'll be paying the bill when the mechanic gets around to working on your car and discovering all the details you already told the service rep. Avoid this hassle by writing a note and either attaching it to the service order or leaving it prominently displayed in the car. Write down everything you can about the problem: What are the symptoms? When do they show up? How does it sound? Feel? Smell? How long has this been going on? How often does it happen? You get the idea.

Don't Forget to Ask

YOURSELF . . .

☐ *Does the service representative listen to what you're saying? Is he or she courteous?*

☐ *Does he or she write down a full description of the problem?*

☐ *Is the waiting room crowded with impatient people waiting to pick up their cars? (Don't expect that you'll get any better or more timely service.)*

☐ *Does the shop look clean? Well run? Well managed?*

☐ *Does the shop have reference books on the shelf? No, you don't want a novice who has to look up where the glove box is, but you do want someone who has all the resources to fix your car right the first time.*

☐ *Does the facility have any complaints filed against it with the local Better Business Bureau?*

THE MECHANIC . . .

☐ *Is the work backed by a written guarantee for at least 30 days? Does it cover parts, labor, or both?*

☐ *Can I get a written estimate before the work begins?*

☐ *Do you provide a courtesy van? A loaner car? A pickup and delivery service? If not, then is there a bus stop near by?*

☐ *Are you certified by any professional organizations? (Certification by the American Automobile Association, the Automotive Service Association, the Automotive Service Excellence, or Automotive Service Councils doesn't guarantee superior service, but they do indicate that the mechanic went to the trouble to pass certain performance requirements.)*

☐ *Do you have experience working with my make and model car?*

☐ *Do you stock all the parts necessary to do the work? Are the parts new, used, or rebuilt?*

You're in the driver's seat. Always insist on a written estimate, including the approximate time the job will take and the approximate cost of the repair; authorize no additional work without your express permission. Don't be pressured into doing any major repairs because the mechanic says he can do it while he's under the hood. The work order should also state whether you will accept rebuilt or used parts, and whether you want the old parts returned. It goes without saying: Never sign a blank work order. If you do you're authorizing the shop to do whatever work they want at whatever price they decide—and you'll pay for it.

Someone's been working on my car . . . If you need major work done to the engine or transmission, see if the car is still covered by the original manufacturer's warranty. If it's covered, the work should be free (or you pay only the labor charges), and in some cases the warranties can be void if you allow someone other than the dealership to work on areas covered by the warranty.

I can take care of that myself, thank you very much. When you bring your car to the dealership for work that's covered by the warranty, expect a lot of pressure to have additional work, such as oil changes, inspections, and tune-ups, done "as long as you're here." The dealership may do an excellent job, but you'll pay more—probably a lot more—than you would at another shop.

Serve yourself. It's easy to check the oil or brake fluid at the service station when you fill up with gas, but don't buy the replacement fluids there unless you want to pay three or four times the price you'd pay at an auto parts store. Save the money and open the bottle yourself.

Know your car's medical history. Before going in for any service, review your car's owner's manual and service record. Expect to get some pressure to buy additional service, so be prepared to know what you need and what you don't.

■ FEEDING YOUR ENGINE:
   BUYING GASOLINE

Some drivers develop fierce brand loyalty when it comes to buying gasoline. Others look for the cheapest price when deciding where to fill up. When debating which kind of gas will quench your car's thirst, there are three things to consider: the octane level, the detergent additives, and the price.

Nothing but the best for my baby. Even if it's a waste of money? Sure, the oil companies tell you to buy the Super-High-Test-Extra-Power-Ultra-Performance premium-grade gasoline, but most cars don't need it. Buying more octane than your car needs is a waste of money and oil (it takes more crude oil to make high-octane gasoline); your car won't run any better or stronger or faster as long as it's in tune. The vast majority of cars run just fine, thank you very much, on regular unleaded (87 octane). Only about 10 percent of all cars need 89 or 91 octane, and these are usually high-performance cars with high-compression engines. Go ahead and read the owner's manual; it will tell you what octane level you need.

This knock-knock is no joke. There is one exception to the lower-is-better rule: Older cars that develop engine knock may need higher-octane gasoline to run their best. These older engines have developed deposits that decrease the compression ratio, and the higher-octane gas helps correct the problem. Engine knock—that rattling and pinging sound coming from your engine, especially when it's climbing a hill or otherwise working hard—can be caused by using fuel that doesn't have enough octane. Don't worry about an occasional bout of knocking, but constant knocking will damage your engine.

Your car can develop hardening of the arteries. Or the automotive equivalent. Gasoline tends to form fuel deposits in the fuel system, which can restrict fuel flow, especially in fuel-injection engines. The cure? Use a gasoline with detergents to unclog the fuel system. You don't necessarily need to buy the pricey premium gasolines; virtually every brand of gasoline adds detergents to all grades of its gasoline, from regular to super-premium. Each brand has its own special recipe or detergent blend; trial and error will help you find the particular blend that works best in your car.

If a station doesn't brag about its special detergents and additives either in the advertising or at the pump, then ask a station attendant if the gasoline has any detergent additives.

Half full or half empty? It could make a difference on a cold winter morning. Keep your tank at least half-full during the winter months; the more fuel in the tank, the less the chances of developing problems due to condensation. The extra air in the empty gas tank allows condensation to build up on the sides. This water can freeze and prevent the engine from starting, and it can cause the gas tank to rust.

Running on empty. It's simply not a great idea. When the fuel tank is low, the gasoline is more likely to pick up any sediment, rust, or water that may be lurking down there and then carry these contaminants into the engine. This is especially important if the car has been sitting a long time. Always fill up by the time the fuel indicator reaches the quarter-tank mark (or before if you're heading off on vacation or won't be driving for a while).

Settle down, settle down. If you have a choice, don't buy gas just after the tanker has refilled the service station's underground tanks. The additional fuel can stir up the sediment at the bottom of the tanks, which could then end up in your engine.

That's Bull

Madison Avenue does its best to convince you that Brand X is vastly superior to Brand Y, but the truth is that all same-octane gasolines are essentially the same until the brand specific additive packages are mixed in. The oil companies don't want you to know it, but most of them have "exchange agreements" that allow other companies to fill up at their terminals. Gasoline is a complex mixture of hundreds of chemicals and components, but the differences don't matter much as long as the fuel meets the same basic specifications. The gasolines don't get their distinctive detergents until they reach the end of the line at the terminal.

Chapter Ten

FOOD FOR THOUGHT

■ FINDING SOMEONE TO CATER TO YOUR DESIRES

Good caterers are like good friends: They understand you. If you pick the right one, your caterer will reflect your fine taste in food preparation and presentation. Pick the wrong one and your affair to remember will best be forgotten.

Whether you're planning a sit-down dinner at a wedding reception for three hundred or an intimate, at-home dinner for six, you'll have to decide how much of the work you want to do for yourself, and how much you want the caterer to do for you. A caterer can simply provide the food, or the caterer can serve as an entertainment contractor, handling equipment rental, staffing, serving and cleaning, and even menu selection and food preparation.

Trust me. You need to find someone you can trust, since you're going to have to delegate a lot of responsibility to the taskmaster. Ideally, you will be able to explain what you want, then the caterer will take over and make it all happen.

Don't grocery shop when you're hungry. But you can visit caterers when you're ready to snack. In addition to asking about foods they specialize in, ask to sample the goods. If you don't like what's being served, your guests probably won't either. Take a look at how the platters are arranged and presented: Does the food look tempting?

Do you have service for 250? No? Then you're

going to have to either rent dishes and glassware yourself, or have the caterer do it for you. Most caterers charge a service fee of about 10 percent when they place the orders for you, even though many rental facilities will deliver and pick up the goods. Leaving these details to the caterer does have several advantages: The caterer may have contacts with the rental outfit and can get equipment in better condition. In addition, if anything goes wrong—you get square tables instead of round ones or you order champagne glasses and tumblers are delivered instead—it's the caterer's problem, not yours. All in all, it gives you less to worry about.

Trivia to Impress Your Friends

Set your timer: Most caterers estimate that a guest eats one hors d'oeuvre every 15 minutes and downs one drink every 30 minutes.

It's the little things that make a difference. And that can make you crazy. Do you have spoons for coffee? Salt and pepper shakers for every table? Communication with the caterer is essential to managing the details. Take nothing for granted: Make sure you and the caterer agree on who does what on every item, however mundane or seemingly obvious.

Is that the bride clearing the dishes? She wouldn't be if she had hired enough service personnel. Your entire event can backfire if you try cutting corners by cutting servers. One server for every ten guests is the basic rule when staffing a dinner, though a buffet usually requires less staff. If you can't afford a sit-down dinner, consider a buffet or cocktails and an hors d'oeuvres display instead.

Living within your means. Know your budget and don't get carried away with the extras. If you're going to need servers and rentals, the food will account for about half the bill. Keep in mind that many caterers calculate the food cost as three times the cost of ingredients, a good reason to avoid costly seafood and meats in favor of money-saving menus rich in vegetables and grains.

Fork it over. When you settle on a caterer and sign a contract, expect to put down a deposit of about 25 percent. You'll be expected to pay the balance on the day of the affair, so keep your checkbook handy. If you cancel the contract, you will usually forfeit the deposit, and if you back

Don't Forget to Ask

After sampling the food but before signing a contract, run over the following questions with a prospective caterer:

☐ *What kind of food do you specialize in?*
☐ *How do you handle special dietary needs or restrictions?*
☐ *Do you have insurance?*
☐ *Who is responsible for setup? Cleanup?*
☐ *Do you supply tables, chairs, dishes, and glassware?*
☐ *Do you supply tablecloths? Napkins? Cutlery? Centerpieces? Salt and pepper shakers, creamers, and other accessories?*
☐ *Do you coordinate the service staff, including bartenders, waiters, and waitresses?*
☐ *How will the service staff be dressed?*
☐ *How will alcohol be handled?*
☐ *Who will coordinate the speeches or entertainment, if any?*
☐ *What is the procedure if more or fewer people show up?*
☐ *How will the payment be handled?*
☐ *What is the procedure for cancellation?*
☐ *Do you have references?*

out at the last minute you may have to pay the full amount, since all the food has been purchased and prepped, if not cooked.

Always room for one more. Round tables allow more flexibility in squeezing an extra guest here or there. If your head count keeps fluctuating, make sure you're renting round tables.

Earthquakes, floods, famine . . . and catering disasters. Face it, forgetting dessert forks so that your guests have to eat wedding cake with their fingers is a bit embarrassing, but it really isn't a tragedy. Plan ahead to avoid miscommunication, then laugh off the things that go wrong.

■ SUPERMARKET SECRETS TO ADD TO YOUR LIST

You don't have to clip coupons to save money in a grocery store. With Americans spending an astounding $382 billion a year on groceries, there are plenty of other ways to trim the fat. Think you're a savvy shopper? Try the following supermarket saving secrets and see how much you can save.

I know we've met, but I can't seem to remember your name. When you go shopping, forget the name brands and buy generic. These no-name brand goods save money; the most popular generic items include paper products, laundry soap, soups, and canned fruits and vegetables.

You've been soaked. If paper towels are on the list, buy the cheapest on the shelf. The ads tout the super-strong, super-absorbent, super-thick towels, but chances are you'll use them for nothing more exotic than drying your hands or wiping up small spills.

Pour yourself a nice tall glass of cold milk. But be sure it comes from a cardboard container, not a translucent plastic jug. The price is usually comparable, but the milk in the plastic container may have a lower vitamin content because it has been exposed to fluorescent lighting. Make every glass of milk count; keep your vitamins intact.

What you see is what you get. Or at least it's what you tend to buy, which is why supermarkets usually place the most expensive items at eye level to encourage impulse purchases. Before reaching for an item, look high and look low to consider your options.

Trivia to Impress Your Friends

A typical single person spends $45 per week on groceries, compared to $92 a week for the typical family of four.

You can't judge a book by its cover. And you can't judge a bargain by the size of a product's container. Instead, refer to the unit-pricing information to determine the price per pound or gallon. You'll be surprised at what you find.

Take a number. Even if you have to wait your turn, you'll probably find that sliced-to-order cold cuts in the deli section are cheaper (and fresher tasting) than the packaged meats. Put them in your own resealable plastic bag when you get home if you want to buy enough lunch meat for an entire week.

Thick skinned. It may be cheaper to buy boneless, skinless chicken breasts than to buy whole breasts and remove the meat yourself. In fact, expect about 45 percent waste when you buy whole breasts and trim and debone them yourself. The processed meat saves time and often saves money, too.

Big Bird is a bargain. Larger turkeys and other birds provide more edible meat per pound than smaller ones. If you'll eat or freeze the leftovers, buy the biggest bird that will fit in your oven.

One price fits all. If produce is sold by the bag, box, or piece, take a minute to put it on the scale. Someone is going to get the Big One, so it might as well be you.

Julia Child versus Betty Crocker. You may be surprised at who the lost-cost victor turns out to be. Contrary to popular wisdom, it's often cheaper to make brownies and other baked goods from mixes rather than from scratch.

■ FRESH FROM THE GARDEN: PICKING PRODUCE

When cruising the vegetable aisle in the grocery store, do you ever eye the unusual fruits and vegetables, wondering what they're called and what to do with them? Here, at last, is a brief list of buying tips that might give you the confidence you need to act on your culinary curiosity.

- **Bitter melon:** Well, for starters, this melon is really a squash. It looks like a five- to eight-inch-long cucumber with acne. Inside, the pink or white pulp should be soaked in saltwater to remove the bitterness. It's used in Asian dishes. Ripeness test: The fruit should be firm and turning slightly yellow.

- **Blood orange:** This sweet orange has dark red pulp and a hint of raspberry or strawberry flavor. It tends to be less acidic than regular oranges. Ripeness test:

The fruit should have a pungent aroma and feel slightly soft.

- **Cherimoya:** The "custard apple" tastes like a combination of pineapple, papaya, and banana—a fruit salad all in one. The creamy white flesh is often added raw to salads, puddings, and pies. Ripeness test: The outside will be brownish-green and it will give slightly when pressed.

- **Kumquats:** These thin-skinned, two-inch citrus fruits are usually popped in the mouth and eaten whole. The fruit is sweet and tart, and is often used in salads as well as in marmalade. Ripeness test: They should be heavy, glossy, and not shriveled.

- **Passion fruit:** If you didn't know better, you might think this fruit was a large egg with shriveled, purple-brown skin. Inside this unattractive exterior lies a pulp surrounding tiny edible seeds that can be used as flavoring in ices, sauces, and punches. Ripeness test: The skin should look old and dimpled.

- **Starfruit:** Officially known as carambolas, the starfruit is usually served in crosswise star-shaped slices as garnish. The flavor can vary from sweet (a sort of orange-pineapple flavor) to sour (a lemon flavor), depending on the type. Ripeness test: The four- to six-inch fruit turns a solid golden color.

■ THE CUTTING EDGE IN CUTLERY

If you've ever tried slicing a tomato or paring an apple with a dull kitchen knife, then you can appreciate the joy of working with fine, sharp cutlery. Whether or not you're an aspiring Julia Child, the right knife can make any culinary task easier.

Isn't carbon the stuff diamonds are made of? You bet, and tough kitchen cutlery is made of high-carbon stainless steel. This material takes and holds an edge well and resists rust and discoloration. Straight stainless steel (sans carbon) is the material used for cheap knives. The good stuff consists of stainless steel mixed with carbon for strength, chromium for shine, vanadium for finish and rust resistance, and molybdenum for flexibility and edge retention.

Keeping you on the edge. A good blade takes on a razor-sharp edge and maintains that edge with just a couple of strokes across a sharpening steel. To recognize a good blade, consider how it was made. Is it stamped or forged? To make a stamped-blade knife, a manufacturer merely cuts the blade out from a flat sheet of steel, then polishes it, sharpens one edge, and slaps on a handle. To produce a forged blade, a manufacturer must go through a number of heating, tempering, sharpening, and hand-finishing stages to transform a block of steel into a single blade. A forged knife has a bolster or collar at the base of the knife, and it has a tapered edge. Top-quality knives are forged, so expect to pay about two to three times more for them than you would for a run-of-the-mill stamped knife.

You can feel the difference. High-quality knives have what's known in the biz as "full tang" construction. What this means is that the metal in the blade actually extends down through the handle. A full-tang knife either shows the edge of metal at the top and bottom of the handle or else it forms a "rat-tail" inside the handle. What makes tangs so important? For one thing there is more weight in the handle, so these knives tend to be better balanced; for another, the stress is distributed across both the handle and blade, so the handle won't have a tendency to loosen with wear.

That's Bull

The amazing Ginsu blade! Strong enough to cut through steel yet gentle enough to glide through a fresh-baked loaf of homemade bread! These claims are true, but what the ads don't tell you is that any decent, properly sharpened knife will perform these same feats.

The secret of the Ginsu knife is its serrated edge, which is not unlike the one on the saw blade in the garage. These knives are serrated both horizontally and vertically, so they can tear their way through almost anything. The problem with these extensive serrations is that it makes a knife virtually impossible to sharpen. In addition, the blades are usually made of inexpensive stamped stainless steel. But, hey, what did you expect when you can get 20 knives for $20?

If you want to show off in the kitchen, learn how to throw a pizza. Don't try to wave your knives through the air and whip them across the sharpening steel like a butcher in a store window. (A notice should be posted at every butcher's shop: "WARNING: These are professionals, do not try this at home.") These guys have used a sharpening steel a few times before; you're apt to lose a finger. Though you'd have to look under a microscope to see them, a knife's edge is actually made up of thousands of tiny cutting teeth. After a few uses, the teeth bend out of place; a couple of swipes across the steel realigns the teeth, without cutting a new edge. To use the steel rod, hold the blade at a 20-degree angle to the steel and with controlled, gentle pressure, pull the blade across the steel from the bolster to the tip. Go all the way to the end or you will end up with dull tips. Alternate between the left and right sides, making about four or five strokes per side.

It's like shaving with a dull razor. If you enjoy the clean, sharp cut of a new razor blade, you'll enjoy working with freshly sharpened cutlery. Sharpeners use either ceramic or diamond-dust imbedded in steel to cut the blade. Ceramic sharpening steel? Sounds strange, but ceramic is not only brittle, it's hard. To keep the sharpeners clean, all you need to do is brush them off periodically and they will last almost forever.

The screwdrivers are in the tool box. The knives are in the kitchen. Remember? If you use your knives to twist screws, pry lids off stubborn cans, or perform other inappropriate tasks, they will respond by snapping in two. Don't be so surprised. The steel used to make knives is relatively brittle. While most high-quality knives come with a manufacturer's warranty—anywhere from one year to a lifetime—they guarantee replacement due to design flaws and defects, not user error.

That's Bull, Too

Some dull-minded cutlery salespeople will try to tell you that knives they're selling won't rust. Perhaps they simply misspoke. There are only two kinds of knives that won't rust: those made of ceramic (which are astronomically expensive), and those coated with titanium nitride, a gold color substance that is extremely hard (and also incredibly expensive). If the knives in question contain steel, they can rust. Many of the knives will do their best to resist rust as long as possible, but under the right conditions, they will succumb.

■ DON'T GET BURNED: CHOOSING COOKWARE

Face it: Any pan can boil water. But if your culinary expertise exceeds the art of the boilin' bag, then you want to make sure your pots and pans are well balanced, easy to clean, and come with comfortable handles and secure lids.

Hot enough to fry an egg on. If you want that egg to cook evenly and without runny spots, you want to choose pots and pans that heat quickly and uniformly. Alas, there is no such thing as the perfect pan. You'll have to accept trade-offs in conductivity, durability, weight, and expense.

■ **Copper cookware:** An excellent conductor of heat but so soft that it needs a gentle touch to keep from getting dented and dinged. Copper also oxidizes and reacts with acidic foods, such as those containing vinegar or lemon juice, so most pans are lined with less reactive tin. If you use the pans often (as you should if you're going to go to the considerable expense to buy copper pots), then you'll have to pay to have them relined every now and then.

■ **Aluminum cookware:** Respectable conductivity at a fraction of the price of copper pots and pans. Aluminum is also a soft metal, but because it's so light the sides can be made thick enough to avoid dents without becoming cumbersome and heavy. Several years ago, some researchers wondered whether there was a link between aluminum cookware and Alzheimer's disease, but there has been no evidence to suggest any health problems associated with pots and pans of this type.

■ **Cast-iron cookware:** This is heavy—a frying pan can easily weigh four pounds or more—and brittle enough to crack if dropped on the floor. But it holds heat extremely well, and if "seasoned" or oiled to prevent rust, it will last almost forever. An added bonus: The cookware does leach trace amounts of iron, which is absorbed by the body. (Just imagine if you cooked liver in a cast-iron pan . . .)

- **Porcelain cookware:** A base layer of steel that has been covered to prevent rust. Steel isn't very good at evenly distributing heat. Any chips in the porcelain will invite rust; and scorched food will never surrender once it's been burned into a porcelain pot.

- **Combination cookware:** Made of two or more metals, one of which is usually stainless steel. Stainless is durable and easy to clean but not a particularly good conductor of heat. By adding a copper or aluminum disk to the bottom of a stainless pan, the manufacturers try to offer the best of both worlds.

Don't just look at the picture. Read the small print on the box of cookware to find out exactly what kind of equipment is stored inside. Many manufacturers make different lines of cookware that look the same but handle differently on the stove. For example, a manufacturer may make one line of pans with copper bottoms, another with aluminum bottoms, and a third with a steel core. Make sure you know what you're buying before you unload the box and strap on your apron.

Ideal for burning dinner. Nonstick coatings really come in handy when there are disasters in the kitchen. Of course, they're designed to keep the food from sticking during regular cooking, but every cook knows that accidents happen—and they can be tough to scour afterward. Virtually every manufacturer has its own version of a nonstick coating; most require the use of plastic or wooden utensils, since the coatings tend to be soft. A couple of nonstick pans are great to have in the kitchen, but you don't necessarily need to buy the entire set. Sometimes you want to use a metal whisk or sharp implement without fear of marring the coating.

That's Bull

Chicken Little has had a field day in the housewares department warning people away from certain types of cookware.

"Be careful! Cast-iron pots and pans will leach iron into the food," hollers Chicken Little. Yup, it will, in small doses that can actually be good for us.

"Be careful! Aluminum pots and pans will leach aluminum into the food," squawks Chicken Little. In amounts 300 to 1,000 times less than the amount in a dose of antacid tablets. While some experts urge you to steer clear of aluminum antacids, the point is that the risk is greatly exaggerated.

"Be careful! Nonstick cookware will leave toxic chemicals in the food," cries You Know Who. Unless the pots are damaged and peeling, the coatings will stay on the pans, and any plastic that makes its way into your body will make its way out in the same form, since the stuff is inert.

In most cases, Chicken Little is playing on health fears to tout a competing type of cookware. Don't fall for the high-pressure sales pitch until you check out health claims with an unbiased source. Time for Chicken Little to jump out of the frying pan and into the fire.

■ TAPPED OUT: BUYING BOTTLED WATER

At the most basic level, gourmet bottled waters are the same as the stuff that pours out of the kitchen tap. It's all H_2O. Brand-name waters have a reputation for purity and wholesomeness, which they must have to justify why consumers should pay as much as ten times the cost of the regular water supplied straight from the faucet. Granted, bottled waters have undergone additional processing, and they may have extra minerals or carbonation added, but when you're thirsty, you probably don't care where your water comes from.

Key Lingo

Though the miracle formula—H_2O—remains the same, there are a number of different types of bottled water.

Drinking water: *Water that has been filtered and disinfected after being drawn from a municipal water system in most cases.*

Natural water: *Bottled spring, mineral, artesian well, or well water that doesn't come from a municipal water supply. The water is filtered and disinfected, but no additional minerals are added.*

Purified water: *Bottled water that is distilled or otherwise processed to meet the federal standards of purification. "Purified" water is free of most minerals; "distilled" water is free of all minerals.*

Mineral water: *Bottled water from a spring or well that contains minerals and trace elements that originate from the water source. The amount of dissolved solids appears on the label.*

Carbonated water: *Sparkling waters that contain carbon dioxide bubbles. Read the labels carefully: "Naturally carbonated mineral water" or "naturally sparkling mineral water" means the carbon dioxide bubbles came from the same source as the water; "carbonated natural mineral water" or "sparkling natural mineral water" means the bubbles were added to natural mineral water; "carbonated or sparkling water" means carbonation was added to refined tap water.*

All that glitters isn't gold. But all that sparkles is carbonated, either naturally or as a result of the production process. In general, sparkling waters are consumed in lieu of another refreshment beverage—a sort of super low-cal cola—and nonsparkling waters are used for regular drinking water as well as for cooking.

Shhh . . . what you don't know won't hurt you. About 75 percent of bottled water comes from protected springs or wells, but what most people don't know is that the remaining 25 percent comes from the regular municipal water supply. That's not to say the bottles are filled directly from the tap; the water is further purified or processed. Don't assume that every bottled water emerged from a natural spring or a cool mountain stream.

Smells like a public swimming pool. Ah, that tell-tale smell of chlorine. You can sometimes smell it in public water supplies but not in bottled waters. The disinfectant used by almost all bottled water companies is ozone, which leaves no aftertaste or smell.

Get the lead out. Lead generally doesn't occur naturally in source waters; it comes from plumbing and pipes. Generally, bottled water has less lead than municipal water systems.

Trivia to Impress Your Friends

Less than one gallon out of every 1,000 from the municipal water supply is poured into a glass and swallowed. The rest goes for washing, bathing, watering, flushing, or just pouring down the drain. Waste not, want not.

■ WHICH BREW FOR YOU?

Beer ranks ahead of coffee, cola, or wine in the world's beverage popularity contest. In fact, only water and tea rank higher. This thirst for beer is nothing new. Beer has been a beverage of choice throughout civilization, even before there were beer commercials on TV. Babylonian and Sumerian clay tablets more than 6,000 years old actually include pictographs showing beer being brewed.

Basic beermaking is quite simple: The brewmeister starts with a starch-rich mash made of grain, rice, or rye. Enzymes turn the starch to sugar. Yeast is added to change the sugar into alcohol during the process known as fermentation. Most European and American beers use "malted" barley that has been steeped in water until it sprouts, then slowly heated to stop the growth. Much of the flavor comes from hops, which can be blended to impart a wide range of flavors.

Lookin' good. Though taste is, of course, the ultimate test, you can tell a lot about a beer by how it looks. Top-notch beer has a long-lasting, dense head about two inches high and small bubbles that rise through the clear amber for several minutes. If the head goes down in seconds this often means the brewer added an artificial foaming agent to the brew—a sign of inferior beer. These signs of excellence let you know, as you raise the glass to your lips, that you're in for something good.

Check for a back-row seat. Beer can be affected by sunlight and exposure to bright fluorescent lights in a supermarket. The light attacks the beer's hops, producing irregular flavors sometimes called "skunkiness." Given the choice, reach for the six-pack in the back row or opt for the brew in the brown- or green-tinted bottles. Beer stays fresh longer in bottles than in cans: Beer in cans begins to deterio-

Key Lingo

There are more than 20,000 brands of beer and 170 styles sold around the world. Here's a rundown on a few of the American favorites:

Ale: A fuller-bodied lager with a stronger hops flavor. Ales are brewed with yeasts that ferment at the top of the fermenting tank. Alcohol content 4 to 5 percent.

Bock: A heavy, but sweet, dark lager with a strong flavor of hops. Alcohol content: 10 to 12 percent.

Brown ale: Sweeter ale, sometimes highly carbonated. Alcohol content: up to 10 percent.

Cream ale: A slight bitter brew, usually consisting of a blend of pale, light ales and lagers. Alcohol content: 5 to 6 percent.

Dark lager: Sweeter than regular lager; the deeper color comes from using roasted barley in the brewing process. Alcohol content: about 5 percent. (Look for coloring on the label; cheap dark lagers contain caramel coloring.)

Malt liquor: An American lager with an alcohol content above 5 percent.

Pilsner or lager: Pale gold, light in body; it's flavored with mild hops and relatively high in carbonation. Lagers are brewed using bottom-fermenting yeasts. Alcohol content: 3.4 to 4.3 percent.

Steam: A sharp lager with a strong hops flavor and full body. This California brew gets its name from the brewing process. Alcohol content: 3.4 to 4.3 percent.

Stout: Dark, strong, and bitter ale; the dark color comes from the highly roasted malt. Alcohol content 5 to 6 percent.

rate after about three months, while bottled beer doesn't show signs of age until about five months.

Just pop the top or snap the cap. Either way, beer should be served at about 40 to 50 degrees F—cold, but not so cold that it will overpower your taste buds. Store beer in a dark, dimly lit area, but don't wait too long to drink it.

Forget that pure mountain stream. No doubt about it: Water is one of the most important ingredients in a good beer (or a bad one for that matter). The primary issue with the water is its mineral content; as a rule, mineral-rich hard water produces better ales and soft water produces better lagers. All the talk about pure water and mountain streams basically boils down to advertising hype. (Surprise!)

On the lighter side. Light beers are the result of a brewmaster's breakthrough in technology. Early on, low-calorie beers were literally watered down. That changed when an enzyme was developed that allowed beer to ferment further, reducing the carbohydrate level (and therefore the calories) and raising the alcohol level. The alcohol level is then adjusted to the same basic level as regular beer.

Trivia to Impress Your Friends

In ancient Egypt, if a young man offered a woman a sip of his beer, they were considered engaged to be married.

As a writer and editor at *Consumer Reports* magazine for seven years, **Winifred Conkling** wrote product reports on subjects ranging from sunscreen to spaghetti sauce. In 1990, she moved to the Washington, D.C., area, where she began work as a freelance writer specializing in consumer and medical topics. She lives with her family in northern Virginia, where she is a member of the board of directors of the Virginia Citizens Consumer Council.